Death and Dying: a Bibliography

1950-1974

Supplement

Volume I

SUICIDE

Death and Dying: a Bibliography

1950-1974

Supplement

Volume I

SUICIDE

by

G. Howard Poteet

and

Joseph C. Santora

The Whitston Publishing Company
Troy, New York
1978

TABLE OF CONTENTS

PREFACE

This bibliography documents the literature of suicide selectively from 1950-1974. The psychology and emotion of suicide, from the point of view of both the subject and survivor—and indeed society—rather than, for example, the forensics, methods, or technical causes of death, govern the inclusions.

It is to be used as a supplement to *Death and Dying, a Bibliography* for 1950-1974 (Whitston, 1976). A further supplement will update the documentation of the literature of both death and dying and of suicide subsequent to 1974; it will also add entries to the 1950-1974 period by more than doubling the number of sources consulted. Those searches, both manual and computer, are currently being conducted.

The work is designed for use by researchers at all levels in sociology, psychology, medicine, education, and allied areas; and comments and suggestions for improvement of coverage or treatment are warmly solicited.

LIST OF ABBREVIATIONS

ABBREVIATIONS	TITLE
AORN J	AORN Journal (Englewood, California)
Abbottempo	Abbottempo (North Chicago)
Acta Sociologica	Acta Sociologica (Copenhagen)
Adolescence	Adolescence (Roslyn Heights, New York)
Ala J Med Sci	Alabama Journal of Medical Sciences (Birmingham)
Am Anthrop	American Anthropologist (Washington)
Am Antiq	American Antiquarian (Worcester, Massachussetts)
Am Bar Ass J	American Bar Association Journal (Chicago)
Am Behav Sci	American Behavioral Scientist (New York)
Am Fam Phys GP	American Family Physician / GP (Kansas City, Missouri)
Am J Epidem	American Journal of Epidemiology (Baltimore)
Am Hist R	American Historical Review (Washington)
Am Imago	American Imago (New York)
Am J Dis Child	American Journal of Diseases of Children (Chicago)
Am J Nurs or AJN	American Journal of Nursing (New York)
Am J Orthopsychiat	American Journal of Orthopsychiatry (New York)
Am J Philol	American Journal of Philology (Baltimore)
Am J Pract Nurs	American Journal of Practical Nursing (Norfolk, Virginia)
Am J Psychiat	American Journal of Psychiatry (Hanover, New Hampshire)
Am J Psychoanal	American Journal of Psychoanalysis (New York)
Am J Psychotherap	American Journal of Psychotherapy (Lancaster)
Am J Pub Health or Am J Public Health	American Journal of Public Health and the Nation's Health (New York)

Am J Soc	American Journal of Sociology (New York)
Am Lit	American Literature (Durham, North Carolina)
Am Merc	American Mercury (New York)
Am Pract	American Practitioner (Philadelphia)
Am Pract Dig Treat or Am Pract & Digest Treat	American Practitioner and Digest of Treatment (New York)
Am Sch Bd J	American School Board Journal (Evanston, Illinois)
Am Soc Rev or Am Sociol R	American Sociological Review (New York)
Ana Clin Sess	American Nurses Association Clinical Sessions (New York)
Ann Intern Med	Annals of Internal Medicine (Philadelphia)
Ann Rev Med	Annual Review of Medicine (Stanford, California)
Antioch Rev	Antioch Review (Yellow Springs, Ohio)
App Ther	Applied Therapeutics (Toronto)
Arch Environ Health	Archives of Environmental Health (Chicago)
Arch Gen Psychiat	Archives of General Psychiatry (Chicago)
Assoc Life Ins Med Dir Am	Association of Life Insurance Medical Directors of America (Boston)
Atlan	Atlantic Monthly (Boston)
Atlas	Atlas (Paris)
Aust Nurs J	Australian Nurses Journal (Sydney, Australia)
Aust NZ J Psychiat	Australian and New Zealand Journal of Psychiatry (Melbourne, Australia)
Bedside Nurse	Bedside Nurse (New York)
Behav Neuropsychiat	Behavioral Neuropsychiatry (New York)
Brit J Addict	British Journal of Addiction (Edinburgh, Scotland)
Brit J M Psychol or Brit J Med Psychol	British Journal of Medical Psychology (London)
Brit J Prev Med Soc	British Journal of Preventive and Social Medicine (London)

Brit J Psychiat or
  Br J Psychiat
	British Journal of Psychiatry
	  (London)

Brit J Soc Clin Psychol	British Journal of Medical Psychology (London)
Brit Med J or Br Med J	British Medical Journal (London)
Bull Hist Med	Bulletin of the History of Medicine (Baltimore)
Bull Menninger Clin	Bulletin of the Menninger Clinic (Topeka)

Bull N Y Acad Med	Bulletin of the New York
	  Academy of Medicine (New
	  York)

Bull Osaka Med Sch
  Suppl
	Bulletin of the Osaka Medical
	  School Supplement (Osaka)

Bull Suicidology	Bulletin of Suicidology (Chevy Chase, Maryland)
Calif Med	California Medicine (San Fran- cisco)
Can J Pub Health	Canadian Journal of Public Health (Toronto)
Can Med Ass J	Canadian Medical Association Journal (Toronto)
Can Ment Health	Canada's Mental Health (Ottawa)
Can Nurs	Canadian Nurse (Ottawa)
Can Psychiat Ass J	Canadian Psychiatric Association Journal (Ottawa)
Cath World	Catholic World (New York)
Chem & Eng	Chemistry and Engineering News (Washington)
Chicago Med	Chicago Medical School Quarterly (Chicago)
Chr Cent or Christian Cent	Christian Century (Chicago)
Chr Today	Christianity Today (Washington)
Class Phil	Classical Philology (Chicago)
Clin Pediat	Clinical Pediatrics (Phila- delphia)
Clin Pharmacol Ther	Clinical Pharmacology Therapeu- tics (St. Louis)

Clin Proc Child Hosp	Clinical Proceedings of the
	  Children's Hospital (Wash-
	  ington)

Col Eng	College English (Urbana, Ill- inois)
Columbia U Forum	Columbia University Forum (New York)

Commentary	Commentary (New York)
Commun Ment Health	Community Mental Health Journal (New York)
Comp Sociol	Comprehensive Sociology (New York)
Compr Psychiatry	Comprehensive Psychiatry (New York)
Conn Health Bull	Connecticut Health Bulletin (Hartford)
Conn Med	Connecticut Medicine (New Haven)
Consultant	Consultant (Philadelphia)
Contemp Ed	Contemporary Education (Terre Haute, Indiana)
Coronet	Coronet (New York)
Cosmo	Cosmopolitan (New York)
Cur	Current (Washington)
Curr Med Drug	Current Medicine and Drugs (London)
Curr Psychiat Ther	Current Psychiatric Therapies (New York)
DM	Disease-a-Month (Chicago)
Delaware Med J	Delaware Medical Journal (Wilmington)
Deutsch Zbl Kranken-pfl	Deutsches Zentralblatt fur Krankenpflege (Stuttgart)
Dis Nerv Syst	Diseases of the Nervous System (Galveston)
Dist Nurs	District Nursing (London)
Dublin R	Dublin Review (London)
Ebony	Ebony (Chicago)
Econ or Economist	Economist (London)
Ed Dig	Education Digest (Ann Arbor)
Ed Resp Rep	Educational Research Reports (Lincoln, Nebraska)
Emerg Med	Emergency Medicine (New York)
Encounter	Encounter (Indianapolis)
Eng Stud	English Studies (Amsterdam)
Epidemiol & Vital Statis Rep	Epidemiology and Vital Statistics Report (Geneva)
Esquire	Esquire (New York)
Eye Ear Nose Throat Monthly	Eye Ear Nose Throat Monthly (Chicago)
Family Health	Family Health Bulletin (Berkeley)

Folia Psychiat Neurol Jap	Folia Psychiatrica Neurologica Japonica (Kyoto)
Forens Sci	Forensic Science (Lusanne)
French R	French Review (New York)
Futurist	Futurist (Washington, D. C.)
Good H	Good Housekeeping (New York)
Geriatrics	Geriatrics (Minneapolis)
Geront Clin	Gerontologia Clinica (Basel)
GP	GP (Kansas City, Missouri)
HSMHA Health Rep	HSMHA Health Reports (London)
Harp Baz	Harper's Bazaar (New York)
Harper	Harper's Monthly Magazine (New York)
Harvard Bsns R	Harvard Business Review (Cambridge)
Hawaii Med J	Hawaii Medical Journal (Honolulu)
Heart and Lung or Heart Lung	Heart and Lung (St. Louis)
Henry Ford Hosp Med J	Henry Ford Hospital Medical Journal (Detroit)
Hispania	Hispania (Worcester, Massachussetts)
Hist Ed Q	History of Education Quarterly (Devon, England)
Hosp or Hospitals	Hospitals (Chicago)
Hosp Commun Psychiat	Hospital and Community Psychiatry (Washington)
Hosp Med	Hospital Medicine (London)
Hosp Pract	Hospital Practice (New York)
Hosp Topics or Hosp Top	Hospital Topics (New York)
Hudson R	Hudson Review (New York)
Human Organ	Human Organization (Lexington, Kentucky)
Human Pathol	Human Pathology (Philadelphia)
Hum Rel or Human Relations	Human Relations (New York)
Ill Med J	Illinois Medical Journal (Chicago)
Image	Image (London)
Imago	Imago (Vienna)
Ind J Med Sci	Indian Journal of Medical Sciences (Bombay)
Ind J Public Health	Indian Journal of Public Health (Calcutta)

Ind Med	Industry Medicine and Surgery (Miami)
Individ Psychol	Individual Psychologist (Chicago)
Infirm	Infirmiere Canadienne (Montreal)
Infirm Fr	Infirmiere Francaise (Paris)
Int Anesth Clin	International Anesthesiology Clinics (Boston)
Int J Addict	International Journal of the Addictions (New York)
Int J Group Psycho-therap	International Journal of Group Psychotherapy (New York)
Int J Soc Psychiat	International Journal of Social Psychiatry (London)
Int Psychiat Clin	International Psychiatry Clinics (Boston)
Internat Soc Sci J	International Social Science Journal (New York)
Isr Ann Psychiat	Israel Annals of Psychiatry and Related Disciplines (Jerusalem)
Ital Affairs	Italian Affairs (Rome)
JAMA	Journal of the American Medical Association (Chicago)
J Abnorm Psychol	Journal of Abnormal Psychology (Washington)
J Abnorm Soc Psych	Journal of Abnormal and Social Psychology (Washington)
J Am Acad Child Psych-iat	Journal of the American Academy of Child Psychiatry (New York)
J Am Coll Health Ass	Journal of the American College Health Association (Ithaca)
J Am Inst Homeop	Journal of the American Institute of Homeopathy (Chicago)
J Am Med Wom Ass	Journal of the American Medical Women's Association (Nashville)
J Amer Geriat Soc	Journal of the American Geriatrics Society (Baltimore)
J Bio Soc Sci	Journal of Biology and Social Sciences (Oxford)
J Ceylon Brit Med	Journal of the Ceylon Branch of the British Medical Association (Colombo)

J Chron Dis	Journal of Chronic Diseases (St. Louis)
J Clin Exp Psycho-path	Journal of Clinical Experimental Psychopathology (Washington)
J Clin Psychol	Journal of Clinical Psychology (Washington)
J Consult Clin Psychol	Journal of Consulting and Clinical Psychology (Washington)
J of Contin Ed Nurs or J Con Ed Nurs	Journal of Continuing Education in Nursing (Thorofare, New Jersey)
J Exist	Journal of Existentialism (New York)
J Fla Med Ass	Journal of the Florida Medical Association (Jacksonville, Florida)
J Forensic Med	Journal of Forensic Medicine (Capetown)
J Gen Psychol	Journal of General Psychology (Provincetown, Massachussetts)
J Gen Psychol or J Genet Psychol	Journal of Genetic Psychology (Provincetown, Massachussetts)
J Health Soc Behav	Journal of Health and Social Behavior (Washington)
J Hist Ideas	Journal of the History of Ideas (New York)
J Ind Med Ass	Journal of the Indiana State Medical Association (Indianapolis)
J Individ Psychol	Journal of Individual Psychology (Chicago)
J Iowa Med Soc	Journal of the Iowa Medical Society (Des Moines)
J Ir Med Ass	Journal of the Irish Medical Association (Dublin)
J Kansas Med Soc	Journal of the Kansas Medical Society
J Ken Med Ass	Journal of the Kentucky Medical Association (Louisville)
J Louisiana Med Soc or J La Med Soc	Journal of the Louisiana Medical Society (New Orleans)
J Maine Med Ass or J Maine M A	Journal of the Maine Medical Association (Brunswick, Maine)

J Marriage & Family	Journal of Marriage and the Family (Minneapolis)
J Med Ass Ala	Journal of the Medical Association of Alabama (Montgomery)
J Med Ass Georgia or J Med Ass Ga	Journal of the Medical Association of Georgia (Atlanta)
J Med Ed	Journal of Medical Education (Washington)
J Med Soc N J	Journal of the Medical Society of New Jersey (Trenton)
J Ment Sci	Journal of Mental Science (London)
J Miss State Med Ass	Journal of the Mississippi State Medical Association (Jackson)
J Nerv Ment Dis	Journal of Nervous and Mental Disease (Baltimore)
J Neuropsychiat	Journal of Neuropsychiatry (Chicago)
J Pers Assess	Journal of Personal Assessment (Durham, North Carolina)
J Person Soc Psych	Journal of Personality and Social Psychology (Washington)
J Phillip Fed Priv Med Pract	Journal of the Philippines Federation of Private Medical Practices (Philippines)
J Pol Econ	Journal of Political Economics (Seikei Ronso)
J Proj Tech or J Proj Tech Pers Assess	Journal of Projective Techniques in Personality Assessment (Burbank, California)
J Psychiat Nurs	Journal of Psychiatric Nursing (Thorofare, New Jersey)
J Psychiat Res	Journal of Psychiatric Research (New York)
J Psychol	Journal of Psychology (Provincetown)
J Psychosom R	Journal of Psychosomatic Research)
J Roy Army Med Corps	Journal of the Royal Army Medical Corps (London)
J S Carolina Med Ass	Journal of the South Carolina Medical Association (Florence)
J Sch Health	Journal of School Health (Columbus)

J Soc Issues	Journal of Social Issues (Ann Arbor, Michigan)
J Soc Psychol	Journal of Social Psychology (New York)
John Hopkins Med J	John Hopkins Medical Journal (Baltimore)
Johper	Journal of Health, Physical Education, Recreation (Washington)
Ladies Home J or Ladies H J	Ladies Home Journal (New (New York)
Lancet	Lancet (London)
Life	Life (New York)
Look	Look (New York)
MS	MS (Marion, Ohio)
Macleans	Maclean's (Toronto)
Mademoiselle	Mademoiselle (New York)
Marquette Med Rev	Marquette Medical Review (Milwaukee)
Md Med J	Maryland Medical Journal (Baltimore)
Med Ann DC	Medical Annals of the District of Columbia (Washington)
Med Bull US Army Europe	Medical Bulletin of the U. S. Army in Europe (Washington)
Med Insight	Medical Insight (New York)
Med J Aust	Medical Journal of Australia (Sydney)
Med Sci Law	Medical Science and the Law (London)
Med Times	Medical Times (Manhasset)
Med World	Medical World (London)
Medicoleg Bull	Medicolegal Bulletin (Richmond)
Medicolegal J or Med Leg J	Medicolegal Journal (Cambridge, England)
Ment Health	Mental Health (London)
Ment Hyg	Mental Hygiene (New York)
Metropolitan Life Ins Co Statis Bul	Metropolitan Life Insurance Company Statistical Bulletin (New York)
Mich Med	Michigan Medicine (East Lansing, Michigan)
Milit Med	Military Medicine (Washington)
Minn Med	Minnesota Medicine (St. Paul)
Mo Med	Missouri Medicine (St. Louis)
Mod Drama	Modern Drama (Lawrence, Kansas)

Mod Lang Q	Modern Language Quarterly (Seattle)
Mt Sinai J Med NY	Mt. Sinai Journal Of Medicine (New York)
NASPA J	NASPA Journal (New York)
NEA J	National Education Association Journal (Washington)
NM	Nurses' Mirror and Midwives' Journal (London)
N Am R	North American Review (Mt. Vernon, New York)
Nat Assn Women Deans & Couns J	National Association of Women Deans and Counselors Journal (Washington)
Nation	Nation (New York)
Nature	Nature (London)
Neb Med J or Neb State Med J	Nebraska State Medical Journal (Lincoln)
Nerv Child	Nervous Child (Baltimore)
Nervenarzt	Nervenarzt (Berlin)
New England Q	New England Quarterly (Brunswick, Maine)
New Eng J Med or N E J Med	New England Journal of Medicine (Boston)
New Leader	New Leader (New York)
New Phys	New Physician (Flossmoor, Illinois)
New Republic	New Republic (Washington)
New Statesman	New Statesman (Washington)
New York Times	New York Times (New York)
New York Times Magazine	New York Times Magazine (New York)
New Yorker	New Yorker (New York)
Newsweek	Newsweek (New York)
19th Cent Fict	19th Century Fiction (Berkeley, California)
Northwest Med or NW Med	Northwest Medicine (Seattle)
Nurs Care	Nursing Care (New York)
Nurs Clin N Amer	Nursing Clinics of North America (Philadelphia)
Nurs Dig	Nursing Digest (Wakefield, Massachussetts)
Nurs Forum or N Forum	Nursing Forum (Chicago)
NM	Nursing Mirror and Midwives' Journal (London)
Nurs Outlk	Nursing Outlook (New York)

Nurs Res	Nursing Research (New York)
Nurs Times or NT	Nursing Times (London)
Nurs '73, '74	Nursing '73, '74 (Jenkintown, Pennsylvania)
NY J Med or NY State J Med	New York State Journal of Medicine (New York)
NZ Nurs J	New Zealand Nursing Journal (Wellington, New Zealand)
Ohio Med J	Ohio State Medical Journal (Columbus)
Pa Med	Pennsylvania Medicine (Harrisburg)
Parents Mag	Parents' Magazine and Better Family Living (New York)
Partisan R	Partisan Review (New Brunswick, New Jersey)
Pediat Clin N Am	Pediatric Clinics of North America (Philadelphia)
Pediatrics or Pediat	Pediatrics (Springfield, Illinois)
Pelican News	Pelican Newsletter (New Orleans, Louisiana)
Penn Med	Pennsylvania Medicine (Lemoyne, Pennsylvania)
Penn Nurs or Pa Nurs	Pennsylvania Nurse (Harrisburg, Pennsylvania)
Percept Mot Skills	Perceptiual and Motor Skills (Missoula, Montana)
Pers Biol Med	Perspectives in Psychiatric Care (Hillsdale, New Jersey)
Phys World	Physician's World (New York)
Plast Recontr Surg	Plastic and Reconstructive Surgery (Baltimore)
Pmla	Periodical of the Modern Language Association (New York)
Police	Police Review (Hagerstown, Maryland)
Pop Sci	Popular Science (Boulder, Colorado)
Popular Govt	Popular Government (Chapel Hill, North Carolina)
Postgrad Med	Postgraduate Medicine (Minneapolis)
Practitioner or Pract	Practitioner (London)

Prairie Rose	Prairie Rose (Bismarck, North Dakota)
Prof Nurs Home	Professional Nursing Home (Minneapolis)
Proc Roy Soc Med	Proceedings of the Royal Society of Medicine (London)
Psychiat Dig	Psychiatry Digest (Northfield, Illinois)
Psychiat Med	Psychiatry and Medical Practice Bulletin (Washington)
Psychiat Q	Psychiatric Quarterly (Utica)
Psychiatry	Psychiatry (Washington)
Psychoanal Rev	Psychoanalytic Review (New York)
Psychol Bull	Psychological Bulletin (Washington)
Psychol Med	Psychological Medicine (London)
Psychol Rep	Psychological Reports (Missoula, Montana)
Psychol Today	Psychology Today (New York)
Psychosomatic	Psychosomatic Medicine (New York)
Psychother Psychosom	Psychotherapy and Psychosomatics (Basel)
PTA Mag	Parent Teachers Association Magazine (Chicago)
Pt Care	Patient Care (Greenwich, Connecticut)
Public Health Rep	Public Health Reports (Washington)
Pulse	Pulse (Philadelphia)
Q J Speech	Quarterly Journal of Speech (New York)
Q J Stud Alcohol	Quarterly Journal of Studies on Alcohol (New Brunswick, New Jersey)
Q Rev DC Nurs Ass	Quarterly Report of the D. C. Nurses' Association (Washington)
RN	Registered Nurse (New York)
Ramp Mag	Ramparts Magazine (San Francisco)
Redbk	Redbook (New York)
Res Phys	Resident Physician (Great Neck, New York)
R Soc Health J	Royal Society of Health Journal (London)

Rev Esc Enferm USP	Revista Espanola de los Enfermedades del Aparato Digestivo
Rev Infirm	Revue de L'Infirmiere et de L'Assistante Sociale (Paris)
R I Med J	Rhode Island Medical Journal (Providence)
Rocky Mount Med J	Rocky Mountain Medical Journal (Denver)
Rural Sociol	Rural Sociology Report (Ames, Iowa)
Russ R	Russiam Review (Stanford, California)
SKF Psychiat	SKF Psychiatrist Report (Philadelphia)
SPEC	Spectator (Philadelphia)
SPEC	Spectator (London)
S A Nurs J	South African Nursing Journal (Pretoria)
S Atlantic Q	South Atlantic Quarterly (Durham, North Carolina)
S Med J	Southern Medical Journal (Birmingham)
Sat Eve Post	Saturday Evening Post (Philadelphia)
Sat R Ed	Saturday Review of Education (New York)
Sat R World	Saturday Review World (New York)
Sch Health Rev	School Health Review (Washington)
Sci Am	Scientific American (New York)
Sci Dig	Scientific Digest (New York)
Sci N L or Sci News Let	Science News Letter (Washington)
Science or Sci	Science (Washington)
Sem Ther	Semaine Therapeutique (Paris)
Seventeen	Seventeen (Radnor, Pennsylvania)
Soc & Econ Admin	Sociology and Economics Administration (London)
Soc Forces	Social Forces (New York)
Soc Prob	Social Problems (New York)
Soc Res	Social Research (New York)
Soc Sci Med	Social Science and Medicine (Oxford)

Sociol & Social Res or Soc & Soc Res	Sociology and Social Research (Los Angeles, California)
Sociol Q	Sociological Quarterly (Carbondale, Illinois)
Southern Med J	Southern Medical Journal (Birmingham)
Sr Schol	Senior Scholastic (New York)
Statis Bull Metrop Life Ins Co	Statistical Bulletin of the Metropolitan Life Insurance Company (New York)
Stud Philol	Studies in Philology (Chapel Hill, North Carolina)
S W Anthrop	South West Journal of Anthropology (Albuquerque)
Tex Med	Texas Medicine (Austin)
Tijdschr Ziekenverpl	Tijdschrift Voor Ziekenverpleging (Amsterdam)
Time	Time (Chicago)
Times Ed Supp	Times Educational Supplement (London)
Tip	Theory into Practice (Columbus, Ohio)
Today's Ed	Today's Education (Washington)
Today's Health	Today's Health (Chicago)
Trans Ass Am Phys	Transactions of the Association of American Physicians (Philadelphia)
Trans Ass Life Insur Med Dir Amer	Transactions of the Association of Life Insurance Medical Directors of America (New York)
Transaction	Transaction (New Brunswick, New Jersey)
Triangle	Triangle (Basel)
Twientieth Cent	Twentieth Century (London)
Una Nurs J	UNA Nursng Journal (Victoria, Australia)
Univ Mi Med Bull	University of Michigan Medical Bulletin (Ann Arbor, Michigan)
Univ Mi Med Cent J	University of Michigan Medical Center Journal (Ann Arbor, Michigan)
Univ Pa Law R	University of Pennsylvania Law Review (Philadelphia)
Univ Q	Universities Quarterly (London)
US Armed Forces M J	U. S. Armed Forces Medical Journal (Washington)

US Naval Aerospace Med Inst	U. S. Naval Aerospace Medical Institute (Pensacola, Florida)
US News	U. S. News and World Report (Washington)
Va Med Mo or Virginia Med Monthly	Virginia Medical Monthly (Richmond)
Va Nurs Q	Virginia Nurses Quarterly (Richmond)
Vet Admin Med Bull	Veterans Administration Medical Bulletin (Washington)
Vital Health Statist	Vital Health Statistics (Washington)
W Med J or Wis Med J	Wisconsin Medical Journal (Madison)
W Virginia Med J	West Virginia Medical Journal (Charleston)
Wall St	Wall Street Journal (New York)
What's New	What's New (New York)
Who Chron	WHO Chronicles (Geneva)
Who Public Health Pap	WHO Public Health Papers (Geneva)
Woman's Home C	Woman's Home Companion (Springfield, Ohio)
World Health	World Health (Geneva)

SUBJECT HEADINGS USED IN THIS BIBLIOGRAPHY

Abortion and Suicide
Adolescence: Attempts
  at Suicide
Adolescence: Boys
Adolescence: Children
Adolescence: College
  Students
Adolescence: Evaluation
  of Suicidal Attempts in
Adolescence: General
Adolescence: Girls
Adolescence: Prevention
  of Suicide During
Adolescence: Reasons
  for Suicide During
Adolescence: Students
Attempted Suicide
Attitudes: Behavior
Attitudes: Ethnic Groups
Attitudes: General
Attitudes: Literature
Attitudes: Myths about
  Suicide
Attitudes: Nurses
Attitudes: Patient
Attitudes: Premeditation
Attitudes: Prevention
Attitudes: Reasons
Attitudes: Reactions to
  Death and Suicide
Attitudes: Religion
Attitudes: Research
Attitudes: Sociology
Attitudes: Solution
Attitudes: Theory
Bereavement
Bibliography: Dynamics
Bibliography: General
Cancer: Suicide as an
  Alternative to Death by
Children: Attempted Su-
  icide
Children: General

Children: Girls
Children: Handicapped
Children: Prediction of
  Suicidal Tendencies in
Children: Prevention of
  Suicide in
Children: Reactions to
  Bereavement
Children: Reasons for
  Suicide by
College Students
Counseling
Cultural Differences:
  Adolescents
Cultural Differences:
  American Indians
Cultural Differences:
  Blacks
Cultural Differences:
  Eskimos
Cultural Differences:
  General
Cultural Differences:
  Hawaii
Drugs" Accidental Poison-
  ing
Drugs: Care and Treatment
Drugs: General
Drugs: Overdose
Drugs: Prevention of Su-
  icide by
Drugs: Sleeping Pills
Drugs: Tranquilizers
Economics
Education: Achievement
Education: General
Education: Students
Education: Teacher
Ethics
Ethnic
Geriatrics: General
Geriatrics: Male Suicides
Geriatrics: Nursing Care

```
U.S.A.:  Alabama
U.S.A.:  Alaska
U.S.A.:  California
U.S.A.:  Colorado
U.S.A.:  Florida
U.S.A.:  General
U.S.A.:  Hawaii
U.S.A.:  Illinois
U.S.A.:  Kansas
U.S.A.:  Louisiana
U.S.A.:  Michigan
U.S.A.:  Nebraska
U.S.A.:  New Hampshire
U.S.A.:  Nevada
U.S.A.:  Oklahoma
U.S.A.:  South Carolina
U.S.A.:  Texas
U.S.A.:  Virginia
U.S.A.:  Washington
U.S.A.:  West Virginia
```

BOOKS

Aldwinckle, Russell F. DEATH IN THE SECULAR CITY: LIFE
AFTER DEATH IN CONTEMPORARY THEOLOGY AND PHILOSOPHY.
Grand Rapids, Michigan: Wm. B. Eerdsman Publishing
Co., 1972.

Allen, Nancy H. SUICIDE IN CALIFORNIA 1960-1970.
Sacramento, California: California Department of Public Health, 1973.

Alvarez, A. THE SAVAGE GOD. London: Weidenfield, 1971.
New York: Random House, 1972.

Barker, A. J. SUICIDE WEAPON. London: Pan Books, 1972.

Bohannan, P. AFRICAN HOMICIDE AND SUICIDE. Princeton,
New Jersey: Princeton University Press, 1960; London:
Oxford, 1960; New York: Atheneum Publishers, 1967.

Bosselman, B. C. SELF-DESTRUCTION. Springfield, Illinois: C. C. Thomas, 1958.

Britt, F. E. FELO-DE-SE: A TREATISE ON THE RECOGNITION
AND PREVENTION OF SUICIDAL BEHAVIOR. New York: Vantage,
1969.

Burnham, J. SUICIDE OF THE WEST. New Rochelle: Arlington
House, 1970.

Cain, A. C. SURVIVORS OF SUICIDE. Springfield, Illinois:
C. C. Thomas, 1972.

Cavan, R. S. SUICIDE. New York: Russell and Russell,
1965.

Chesser, Eustace. LIVING WITH SUICIDE. London: Hutchin-
son, 1967.

Choron, J. SUICIDE. New York: Scribner, 1972.

Church of England General Assembly. OUGHT SUICIDE TO BE
A CRIME? A DISCUSSION OF SUICIDE, ATTEMPTED SUICIDE
AND THE LAW. London: Church of England Information
Office, 1959.

Cioran, E. M. THE NEW GODS. New York: Quadrangle/The
New York Times Book Co., 1974.

Clark, A. A. G. SUICIDE EXCEPTED. New York: Macmillan
Faber, 1955.

Coleman, J. M., et al. LIFE AND DEATH: THEIR SOCIAL
DEFINITIONS. New York: Glanville Publishing, 1973.

Daniel, R. SUICIDE CAN BE MURDER. London: Wright and
Brown, 1957.

Desmond, H. SUICIDE FLEET. London: Wright and Brown,
1959.

Douglas, Jack D. SOCIAL MEANINGS OF SUICIDE. Princeton,
New Jersey: Princeton University Press, 1967.

Dublin, Louis I. SUICIDE: A SOCIOLOGICAL AND STATISTICAL
STUDY. New York: Ronald Press, 1963.

Durkheim, E. SUICIDE. New York: Free Press, 1966.

--- SUICIDE: A STUDY IN SOCIOLOGY. Boston: Routledge
and Kegan, 1952.

Eckert, William G., et al. SUICIDE, 1968.

Ellis, E. R., et al. TRAITOR WITHIN. Toronto: Double-
day, 1961.

Elwin, V. MAFIA MURDER AND SUICIDE. New York: Oxford,
1950.

Ettlinger, R. W., et al. ATTEMPTED SUICIDE. n.p.:
Munksgaard, 1956.

Farber, Leslie H. THE WAYS OF THE WILL: ESSAYS TOWARD
A PSYCHOLOGY AND PSYCHOPATHOLOGY OF WILL. London:
Constable, 1966.

2

Farber, Maurice L. THEORY OF SUICIDE. New York: Funk and Wagnalls, 1968.

Farberow, Norman L. BIBLIOGRAPHY ON SUICIDE AND SUICIDE PREVENTION, 1897-1957. Washington, D. C.: U. S. National Institute of Mental Health, 1959.

--- BIBLIOGRAPHY ON SUICIDE AND SUICIDE PREVENTION, 1958-1970. Washington, D. C.: U. S. National Institute of Mental Health, 1972.

--- ,et al. THE CRY FOR HELP. New York: McGraw Hill, 1961.

Fedden, J. R. SUICIDE, A SOCIAL AND HISTORICAL STUDY. n.p.: B. Blom, 1972.

Finch, S. M., et al. ADOLESCENT SUICIDE. Springfield, Illinois: C. C. Thomas, 1971.

Fisher, S. A. SUICIDE AND CRISIS INTERVENTION. NewYork: Springer Publishers, 1973.

Fisher, V. SUICIDE OR MURDER? Chicago: Swallow, 1962.

Flescher, J. SUICIDE-- MAN'S FATE? New York: DTRB Eds., 1971.

Friedman, P. ON SUICIDE. New York: International Universities Press, 1967.

Gibbs, J. P. SUICIDE. New York: Harper, 1968.

---, et al. STATUS INTEGRATION AND SUICIDE. Eugene, Oregon: University of Oregon Press, 1964.

Giddens, A. THE SOCIOLOGY OF SUICIDE. London: Cass, 1971.

Grollman, Earl A. SUICIDE: PREVENTION, INTERVENTION, POST-VENTION. Boston: Beacon Press, 1971.

Hafen, B. Q., et al. SELF DESTRUCTIVE BEHAVIOR. Minneapolis: Burgess Publishing Co., 1972.

Hendin, H. BLACK SUICIDE. New York: Basic Books, 1969; London: Penguin, 1970.

3

---SUICIDE AND SCANDINAVIA: A PSYCHOANALYTIC STUDY OF CULTURE AND CHARACTER. New York: Grune and Stratton, 1964; Toronto: Doubleday, 1965.

Henry, A. F., et al. SUICIDE AND HOMICIDE. New York: Macmillan, 1964.

Herzog, Edgar. PSYCHE AND DEATH. New York: Putnam, 1967.

Hillman, James. SUICIDE AND THE SOUL. New York: Harper, 1964.; London: Hodder and Stoughton, 1964.

Israel Central Bureau of Statistics. SUICIDES AND ATTEMPT-FD SUICIDES IN ISRAEL (1960-1966). Jerusalem: Central Bureau of Statistics, 1969.

Jacobs, J. ADOLESCENT SUICIDE. London: Wiley, 1971.

Kobler, A. L., et al. THE END OF HOPE. New York: Macmillan, 1964.

Landsberg, P. L. MORAL PROBLEM OF SUICIDE. New York: Philosophical Library, 1953; London: Rockliffe, 1953.

Lee, W. C. SUICIDE TRAIL. n.p.: Lenox Hill Press, 1972.

Leonard. C. V. UNDERSTANDING AND PREVENTING SUICIDE. Springfield, Illinois: C. C. Thomas, 1967.

Lester, D. WHY PEOPLE KILL THEMSELVES. Springfield, Illinois: C. C. Thomas, 1972.

Lester, G., et al. SUICIDE: THE GAMBLE WITH DEATH. Englewood Cliffs, New Jersey: Prentice-Hall, 1971.

Lum, D. RESPONDING TO SUICIDAL CRISIS: FOR CHURCH AND COMMUNITY. Grand Rapids, Michigan: Wm. B. Eerdmans Publishing Co., 1974.

McCormick, D. THE UNSEEN KILLER. Philadelphia: W. B. Saunders Co., 1964.

McCulloch, W. SUICIDAL BEHAVIOR. Elmsford, New York: Pergamon, 1972.

Mannes, M. LAST RIGHTS. New York: Wm. Morrow and Co., Inc., 1974.

Maris, R. W. SOCIAL FORCES IN URBAN SUICIDE. Homewood, Illinois: Dorsey Press, 1969.

Masaryk, T. G. SUICIDE AND THE MEANING OF CIVILIZATION. Chicago: University of Chicago Press, 1970.

Meaker, M. SUDDEN ENDINGS. Garden City, New York: Double-day, 1964.

Meer, Fatima. SUICIDE IN DURBAN: A STUDY OF SUICIDE PATTERNS AMONG INDIANS, EUROPEANS, AFRICANS, AND COLOUREDS. Durban: University of Natal, 1964.

Meerloo, A. M. SUICIDE AND MASS SUICIDE. New York: Grune and Stratton, 1962; New York: E. P. Dutton, 1968.

MENTAL DISORDERS SUICIDE. Cambridge: Harvard University Press, 1972.

Mental Health Research Fund. DEPRESSIONS AND SUICIDE. London: The Fund, 1962.

Motto, Jerome A., et al. STANDARDS FOR SUICIDE PREVENTION AND CRISIS CENTERS. New York: Behavioral Publishers, 1974.

Neuringer, Charles. PSYCHOLOGICAL ASSESSMENT OF SUICID-AL RISK. Springfield, Illinois: C. C. Thomas, 1974.

New York, New York Board of Correction. REPORT ON PRISON SUICIDES AND URGENT RECOMMENDATIONS FOR ACTION. New York: Board of Correction, 1972.

Niswander, G. D., et al. A PANORAMA OF SUICIDE. Spring-field, Illinois: C. C. Thomas, 1973.

Ognall, L. H. SUICIDE CLAUSE. London: Collins, 1968.

Pederson, D., et al. GOING SIDEWAYS. New York: Hawthorne Books, 1974.

Pretzel, P. W. UNDERSTANDING AND COUNSELING THE SUICIDAL PERSON. Nashville, Tennessee: Abington Press, 1972.

Randall, A. A. SUICIDE PASSAGE. London: Allen, 1968.

Resnik, H. L. P. SUICIDAL BEHAVIORS: DIAGNOSIS AND
MANAGEMENT. Boston: Little, Brown and Co., 1968.

---, et al. SUICIDE PREVENTION IN THE SEVENTIES.
Washington, D.C.: National Institute of Mental Health
Center for Studies of Suicide Prevention, 1973.

Retterstol, N. LONG TERM PROGNOSIS AFTER ATTEMPTED
SUICIDE. Springfield, Illinois: C.C. Thomas, 1970.

THE RIGHT TO DIE: DECISION AND DECISION MAKERS. n. p. :
J. Aronson, 1974.

Sainsbury, P. SUICIDE IN LONDON: AN ECOLOGICAL STUDY.
New York: Basic Books, 1956: London: Chapman, 1955.

St. John - Stevas, et al. THE RIGHT TO LIFE. London: Hodder and Stoughton, 1963; New York: Holt, 1964.

Seiden, Richard H. SUICIDE AMONG YOUTH: A REVIEW OF THE
LITERATURE, 1900-1967. Washington, D. C.: National
Institute of Mental Health, 1969.

Seward, J. HARA-KIRI. London: Tuttle, 1967; Englewood
Cliffs, New Jersey, Prentice-Hall, 1968.

Shneidman, E. S. DEATH AND THE COLLEGE STUDENT. New
York: Behavioral Publications, 1972.

--- ESSAYS IN SELF-DESTRUCTION. New York: Science House,
Inc., 1967.

---, et al. CLUES TO SUICIDE. New York: McGraw-Hill,
1963.

---, et al. PSYCHOLOGY OF SUICIDE. New York: Science
House, 1970.

Stengel, E. S. SUICIDE AND ATTEMPTED SUICIDE. Harmonds-
worth: Penguin Books, 1964; New York: International
Publications, 1965.

---, et al. ATTEMPTED SUICIDE. London: CHapman, 1958.

Stern, D. THE SUICIDE ACADEMY. New York: McGraw Hill,
1968; London: W. H. Allen, 1970.

Stone, H. W. SUICIDE AND GRIEF. Philadelphia: Fortress Press, 1972.

Thakur, U. THE HISTORY OF SUICIDE IN INDIA. n. p. : Munshi Ram, 1963.

Tombs, T. P. TRENDS IN SUICIDAL BEHAVIOR. Edmonton, Canada: Anglican Church of Canada, Diocese of Edmonton, Council of Social Service, 1965.

United States National Office of Vital Statistics. DEATH RATES BY AGE, RACE, AND SEX, UNITED STATES 1900-1953. Washington, D. C.: Office of Vital Statistics, 1956.

--- DEATH RATES FOR SELECTED CAUSES BY AGE, COLOR, AND SEX, UNITED STATES AND EACH STATE, 1949-1951. Washington, D. C. : Office of Vital Statistics, 1959.

Usher-Wilson, R. N. SUICIDE OR ADORATION. New York: Vantage, 1972.

Varah, Edward C. THE SAMARITANS: TO HELP THOSE TEMPTED TO SUICIDE OR DESPAIR. London: Constable, 1965.

Verkko, V. K. HOMICIDES AND SUICIDES IN FINLAND AND THEIR DEPENDENCE ON NATIONAL CHARACTER. n.p.: Stechert-Hafner, 1951.

Wallace, S. E. AFTER SUICIDE. New York: John Wiley and Sons, Inc., 1973.

Webster, D. B. SUICIDE SPECIALS. Harrisburg, Pennsylvania: Stackpole Co., 1957.

West, Donald J. MURDER FOLLOWED BY SUICIDE: AN INQUIRY CARRIED OUT FOR THE INSTITUTE OF CRIMINOLOGY, CAMBRIDGE. London: Heinemann, 1965; Cambridge: Harvard, 1966.

Wolff, K. PATTERNS OF SELF DESTRUCTION: DEPRESSION AND SUICIDE. Springfield, Illinois: C. C. Thomas, 1970.

Yap, P. M. SUICIDE IN HONG KONG. Hong Kong: Hong Kong University Press, 1958; London: Oxford, 1959.

SUBJECT INDEX

ABORTION AND SUICIDE
  "Abortion and suicidal behaviors: observations on the
  concept of endangering the mental health of the
  mother," by H. L. Resnik, et al. MENT HYG 55:10-
  20, January, 1971

ADOLESCENCE: ATTEMPTS AT SUICIDE
  SEE PARASUICIDE: ADOLESCENTS

ADOLESCENCE: BOYS
  SEE STUDENTS

ADOLESCENCE: CHILDREN
  SEE CHILDREN

ADOLESCENCE: COLLEGE STUDENTS
  SEE STUDENTS: COLLEGE

ADOLESCENCE: EVALUATION OF SUICIDAL ATTEMPTS IN
  "Evaluation and treatment of suicide-prone youth," by
  M. King. MENT HYG 55:344-350, July, 1971.

ADOLESCENCE: GENERAL
  "Adolescent suicide and premarital sexual behavior,"
  by D. J. Lester. J SOC PSYCHOL 82:31-32, October,
  1970.

  "Adolescent suicidal behavior," by E. J. Stanley, et
  al. AM J ORTHOPSYCH 40:87-96, January, 1970.

  "Art therapy with a 12 year old who witnessed suicide
  and developed school phobia," by I. Jakab, et al.
  PSYCHOTHER PSYCHOSOM 17:309-324, 1969

8

"A program for suicidal patients," by N. Tallent, et al. AJN 66:2014-2016, September, 1966.

"Psychological 'biopsy' in self-poisoning of children and adolescents," by M. S. McIntire, et al. AM J DIS CHILD 126:42-46, July, 1973.

"Some typical patterns in the behavior and background of adolescent girls who attempt suicide," by A. Schrut. AM J PSYCHIAT 125:69-74, July, 1968.

"Student suicide at Oxford University. The relevance of a university health service to student mental health," by J. L. Lyman. STUDENT MED 10:218-234, December, 1961.

"Student suicide: fact or fancy?" by H. B. Bruyn, et al. J AM COLL HEALTH ASS 14:69-77, December, 1965.

"A study of suicide attempts by male and female university students," by L. R. Carmen, et al. INT PSYCHIAT CLIN 7:181-199, 1970.

"The suicidal adolescent -- the expendable child," by J. C. Sabbath. J AMER ACAD CHILD PSYCHIAT 8:272-289, April, 1969.

"Suicidal adolescents and children," by A. Schrut. JAMA 188:1103-1107, June 29, 1964.

"Suicidal attempts in adolescent girls. A preliminary study," by J. Bigras, et al. CANAD PSYCHIAT ASS J 11: SUPP: 275-282, 1966.

"Suicidal attempts in children," by R. H. Lawler, et al. CANAD MED ASS J 89:751-754, October 12, 1963.

"Suicidal behavior among college students," by M. L. Peck, et al. HSMHA HEALTH REP 86:149-156, February, 1971.

"Suicidal behavior as child psychiatric emergency. Clinical characteristics and follow-up results," by A. Mattson, et al. ARCH GEN PSYCHIAT (CHICAGO) 20: 100-109, January, 1969.

"Campus tragedy: a study of student suicide," by R. H. Seiden. J ABNORM PSYCHOL 71:389-399, December, 1966.

"Cases of probable suicide in young persons without obvious motivation," by A. W. Stearns. J MAINE M A 44:16-23, January, 1953.

"Causal factors in suicidal attempts by male and female college students," by G. B. Blaine, et al. AM J PSYCHIAT 125:834--37, December, 1968.

"Characteristics of suicides in Japan, especially of parent-child double suicide," by K. O'Hara. AM J PSYCHIAT 120:382-385, October, 1963.

"Children and adolescents who attempt suicide," by J. D. Teicher. PED CLIN N AM 17:687-696, August, 1970.

"Children's disturbed reactions to parent suicide," by A. C. Cain, et al. AM J ORTHOPSYCHIAT 36:873-880, October, 1966.

"Chronic disease in former college students: implications for college health programs," by R. S. Paffenbarger, Jr. J AM COLL HEALTH ASS 16:51-55, October, 1967.

"Clinical studies of attempted suicide in childhood," by R. S. Lourie. CLIN PROC CHILD HOSP (WASH) 22: 163-173, June, 1966.

"Deaths in a youth program," by E. J. Faux, et al. MENT HYG 54:569-571, October, 1970.

"Depression and suicide in children and adolescents," by J. W. King. GP 36:95-104, March, 1969.

"Detection and management of the suicidal patient," by R. S. Mintz. DM 1961:1-38, July, 1961.

"Evaluating suicide impulse in university setting," by V. W. Jensen. LANCET 75:441-444, October, 1955.

"Family treatment approaches to suicidal children and adolescents," by G. C. Morrison, et al. J AM ACAD CHILD PSYCHIAT 8:140-153, January, 1969.

"Fetal suicide," by D. Lester. JAMA 209:1367. September 1, 1969.

"Hanging in childhood," by J. H. Salmon. JAMA 201:204-205, July 17, 1967.

"I want out: teens who threaten suicide," by H. Pollack. TODAY'S HEALTH 49:32-34+, January, 1971.

"Intropunitiveness in suicidal adolescents," by M. Levenson, et al. J PROJ TECH PERS ASSESS 34:409-411, October, 1970.

"Latency-age children who threaten or attempt to kill themselves," by W. C. Ackerly. J AM ACAD CHILD PSYCHIAT 6:242-261, April, 1967.

"Management of adolescent suicide attempts," by D. W. Cline. MINN MED 56:111-113, February, 1973.

"MMPI scores of old and young completed suicides," by D. Lester. PSYCHOL REP 28:146, February, 1971.

"Modes of occurrence of accidental ingestions in children and a suicide attempt," by H. Jacobziner, et al. NY J MED 60:426-429, February 1, 1960.

"Portrait of a teen-age suicide," SCI N 102:423, December 30, 1972.

"Prevalence of suicidal ideation and behavior among basic trainees and college students," by D. E. Flinn, et al. MILIT MED 137:317-320, August, 1972.

"Prevention of suicide," by V. Bloom. CURR PSYCHIAT THER 10:105-109, 1970.

"Problem solving behavior in suicidal adolescents," by M. Levenson, et al. J CONSULT CLIN PSYCHOL 37:433-436, December, 1971.

"Suicidal behavior in children," by C. R. Shaw, et al. PSYCHIATRY 28:157-168, May, 1965.

"Suicidal children -- management," by K. Glaser. AM J PSYCHOTHER 25:27-36, January, 1971.

"Suicidal ideation and behavior in youthful nonpsychiatric populations," by C. V. Leonard, et al. J CONSULT CLIN PSYCHOL 38:366-371, June, 1972.

"Suicidal intent in adolescence: a hypothesis about the role of physical illness," by S. Weinberg. J PEDIAT 77:579-586, October, 1970.

"Suicidal tendencies among college students," by L. J. Braaten, et al. PSYCHIAT Q 36:665-692, October, 1962.

"Suicide among college students," by M. Ross. AM J PSYCHIAT 126:220-225, August, 1969.

"Suicide among teenagers," SCI DIG 60:42, August, 1966.

"Suicide among university students," by L. Sims, et al. J AM COLL HEALTH ASS 21:336-338, April, 1973.

"Suicide among young persons. A review for its incidence and causes, and methods of its prevention," by H. C. Faigel. CLIN PEDIAT (PHILA) 5:187-190, March, 1966.

"Suicide and adolescence," by J. P. Miller. ADOLESCENCE 10:11-24, Spring,1975.

"Suicide and attempted suicide in children and adolescents," by R. S. Lourie. TEXAS MED 63:58-63, November, 1967.

"Suicide and attempted suicide in children and adolescents," by J. H. Yacoubian, et al. CLIN PROC CHILD HOSP DC 25:325-344, December, 1969.

"Suicide and college," NEWSWEEK 50:78, July 29, 1957.

"Suicide and sibling position," by D. Lester. J IND-
IVID PSYCHOL 26:203-204, November, 1970.

"Suicide and suicidal attempts in children and adolescents," LANCET 2:847-848, October 17, 1964.

"Suicide and suicidal attempts in children and adolescents," by J. M. Toolan. AM J PSYCHIAT 118:719-724,
February, 1962.

"Suicide attempt by a ten-year-old after quadruple
amputations," by H. L. Resnik. JAMA 212:1211-1212,
May 18, 1970.

"Suicide attempts in a population pregnant as teenagers," by I. W. Gabrielson, et al. AM J PUBLIC HEALTH
60:2289-2301, December 1970.

"Suicide in adolescence," by B. H. Balser. AM J PSYCH-
IAT 116:400-404, November, 1959.

"Suicide in adolescence," by A. P. Perlstein NY J MED
66:3017-3020, December 1, 1966.

"Suicide in adolescents," by W. D. Schechter, et al.
POSTGRAD MED 47:220-223, May, 1970.

"Suicide in childhood and adolescence," by M. Clark.
NEA J 53:32-33+, November, 1964.

"Suicide in children," by B. Y. O'Dell. PARENTS MAG
44:58-59+, January, 1969.

"Suicide in children and adolescents," by H. Bakwin.
J AM MED WOM ASSN 19:489-491, June, 1964.

"Suicide in children and adolescents," by S. V. Grandis.
MEDICOLEG BULL 172:1-5, August, 1967.

"Suicide in children and adolescents," by J. M. Lampe.
J SCHL HEALTH 34:390-391, October, 1964.

"Suicide in children and adolescents," by W. M. Lordi.
VA MED MON 98:209-213, April, 1971.

ADOLESCENCE: GENERAL

"Suicide problems in children and adolescents," by R.
E. Gould. AM J PSYCHOTHER 19:228-246, April, 1965.

"Suicide rates amomg high school and college students,"
NEW YORK TIMES 39:1, April 26, 1968.

"Suicide risk in teenage pregnancy," BR MED J 2:602,
June 12, 1971.

"Suicide: the adolescent: a special case," by Sabbath.
EMERG MED 1:40+, April, 1969.

"Suicide threats and attempts in young: psychologic
management," by D. Powers. AM PRACT & DIGEST TREAT 7:
1140-1143, July, 1956.

"Survey of suicide counseling available to students in
metropolitan Richmond," by P. J. Johnson, et al.
PUBLIC HEALTH REP 84:118-120, February, 1969.

"Teen-age suicide," by H. Bakwin. ARCH ENVIRON HEALTH
12:276-278, March, 1966.

"Teen-age suicide," by D. Carlinsky. SR SCHOL 102:13-
15, February 7, 1974.

"Thirteen adolescent male suicide attempts. Dynamic
considerations," by N. L. Margolin, et al. J AM ACAD
CHILD PSYCHIAT 7:296-315, April, 1968.

"Today's students. Suicide among students and its prevention," by R. Fox. R SOC HEALTH J 91:181-185,
July-August, 1971.

"Treatment and prevention of poisoning," BR MED J 4:
787-788, December 28, 1968.

"Youthful suicides," NEWSWEEK 77:70-71, February 15,
1971.

ADOLESCENCE: GIRLS
"Bullying one reason for girl's death: Southampton
report," TIMES ED SUPPL 3064:6-7, February 15, 1974.

ADOLESCENCE: GIRLS

"Problems and encounters of a suicidal adolescent girl,"
by I. Babow, et al. ADOLESCENCE 7:459-478, Winter,
1972.

"Suicide attempts in a population pregnant as teenagers,"
by I. W. Gabrielson, et al. AM J PUBLIC HEALTH 22:
89--301, December, 1970.

"Tragedy of young girl suicides," by A. McMann. COSMO
140:78-80, June, 1956.

"Young people, suicide and the need for attention:
work of the Samaritans in Great Britain," PSYCHOL
TODAY 7:88, March, 1974.

"Youngsters (especially girls) and suicide," by D.
Lester. MENT HYG 54:568, October, 1969.

ADOLESCENCE: PREVENTION OF SUICIDE DURING
SEE PREVENTION

ADOLESCENCE: REASONS FOR SUICIDE DURING
SEE MOTIVATION

ADOLESCENCE: STUDENTS
SEE EDUCATION

ATTEMPTED SUICIDE
SEE PARASUICIDE

ATTITUDES: BEHAVIOR
"Depression, despair and suicide," by E. Maycock. TIMES
ED SUP 2647:407, February 11, 1966.

"Divergencies between attitudes towards life and death
among suicidal, psychosomatic, and normal hospitalized
patients," by C. Neuringer. J CONSULT CLIN PSYCHOL
32:59-63, February, 1968.

"Factors related to continued suicidal behavior in
dyadic relationships," by R. A. Harris. NURS RES
15:72-75, Winter, 1966.

"Suicidal behavior, " by S. Acker. INFIRM FR 148:9-11,
October, 1973.

ATTITUDES: BEHAVIOR

"Suicidal behavior," by J. Wilkins. AM SOC R 32:286-298, April, 1967.

"Suicidal behavior in men and women," by D. Lester. MENT HYG 53:340-345, July, 1969.

"Suicidal tendencies," SCI N 90:513, December 17, 1966.

"Temptation of giant despair," by P. Hobsbaum. HUDSON R 25:597-612, Winter, 1972-1973.

ATTITUDES: ETHNIC GROUPS
SEE ALSO OTHER COUNTRIES, CULTURAL DIFFERENCES
"Cultural factors in suicide of Japanese youth with focus on personality," by M. Iga. SOCIOL & SOCIAL RES 46:75-90, October, 1961.

"Death under the cherry blossom (Japanese suicide rate)," ECON 187:324+, April 26, 1958.

"Notes on Eskimo patterns of suicide," by A. Leighton, et al. S W ANTHROP 11:327-338, Winter, 1955.

"On suicide rate differentials in Tulsa," by B. Brenner. AM SOCIOL R 25:265-266, April, 1960.

"Status integration and suicide in Ceylon," by J. P. Gibbs, et al. AM J SOCIOL 64:585-591, May, 1959.

"Suicide and culture in Fairbanks: a comparison of three cultural groups in a small city of interior Alaska," by M. Parkin. PSYCHIAT 37:60-67, February, 1974.

"Suicide, homicide, and social structure in Ceylon," by J. H. Strauss. AM J SOCIOL 58:461-469, March, 1953.

"Suicide in Canada -- trends and preventive aspects," by F. A. Allodi, et al. CAN MENT HEALTH 21:15-16, September-October, 1973.

"Suicides in Los Angeles and Vienna. An intercultural study of two cities," by Farberow, et al. PUB HEALTH REP (WASH) 84:389+, May, 1969.

ATTITUDES: ETHNIC GROUPS

"Symbolic suicide: Nguyen Tuong Tam," NEWSWEEK 62:
43-44, July 22, 1963.

ATTITUDES: GENERAL
"Alternative to suicide," TIME 97:48, April 26, 1971.

"And certain thoughts through my head," by B. Fallon.
AJN 72:1257-1259, July, 1972.

"Another look at suicide," by Wallace. NM 129:27+, November 21, 1969.

"Decision to die," by S. Alexander. LIFE 56:74-76+,
May 29, 1964.

"Do they really want to die?" by K. B. Murphy. TODAY'S
HEALTH 43:48-49+, April, 1965.

"Easier on suicides," TIME 78:23, August 18, 1961.

"Freedom to choose one's death," by J. A. M. Meerloo.
NATION 200:344-345, March 29, 1965.

"How do you stand?" by DeSales. AORN 6:40+, October,
1967.

"How guilty am I?" NEWSWEEK 47:61, February 20, 1956.

"Human voice means more: means of protest," TIME 86:
118, November 19, 1965.

"I'm going to kill myself," by A. Hamilton. SCI DIG
54:57-63, September, 1963.

"I don't want any friends," LIFE 28:43, May 22, 1950.

"Killer we don't talk about," by W. S. Griswold. POP
SCI 173:129-131, November, 1958.

"Let's talk about suicide," by Clark. RN 23:58+, November, 1960.

"Misunderstood matter of suicide," by J. Horn. PSYCHOL
TODAY 8:138, December, 1974.

ATTITUDES: GENERAL

"On the love of suicide," by R. Winegarten. COMMENTARY
54:29-34, August, 1972.

"The question of suicide," IMAGE 11:27+, June, 1969.

"Revenge on life," by M. Howard. SPEC 201:280, August
29, 1958.

"Sensitivity toward suicide," CHR TODAY 13:21-22, July
18, 1969.

"Some myths about suicide," SCI DIG 44:36, November,
1958.

"Suicide," by Wallace. NM 127:16, August 30, 1968.

"Suicide: a new attack against an old killer," by J.
Star. LOOK 30:60+, August 23, 1966.

"Suicide is dangerous," by L. David. CORONET 37:157-160,
February, 1955.

"Thinking of suicide?" by H. Thompson. AM MERCURY 77:
125-127, December, 1953.

"Wanting to die. Case conference from Chester City
Hospital," NT 62:1253-1258, September 22, 1966.

"What about suicide?" AMERICA 103:591, September 3, 1960.

"When life becomes intolerable," EMERG MED 4:25-28, January, 1972.

"Why people can't take it," by F. R. Schreiber, et al.
SCI DIG 56:66-69, September 9, 1964.

"Will to die," NEWSWEEK 38:50, August 6, 1951.

ATTITUDES: LITERATURE
SEE LITERATURE

ATTITUDES: MYTHS ABOUT SUICIDE
"Explode myths on suicide," by A. J. Snider. SCI DIG
29:36-37, May, 1951.

ATTITUDES: NURSES
  SEE ALSO: NURSING
  "Attitude of nurses to patients who attempted suicide,"
    by J. Spies. S A NURS J 38:28, May, 1971.

  "Attitudes to suicidal patients," by Luke. NM 127:15,
    August 30, 1968.

  "Attitudes toward death. A comparison of nursing stud-
    ents and graduate nurses," by S. Golun, et al. NURS
    RES 20:503-508, November-December, 1971.

  "Attitudes toward death held by staff of a suicide pre-
    vention center," by D. Lester. PSYCHOL REP 28:650,
    April, 1971.

  "Attitudes toward death in patients following suicide
    attempts," by G. Irle. NERVENARZT 39:255-260, June,
    1968.

  "Attitudes toward death of NP patients who have attempt-
    ed suicide," by I. M. Cash, et al. PSYCHOL REP 26:
    879-882, June, 1970.

  "Intensive care: a crisis situation," by Woodforde. AUST
    NURS J 65:50+, March, 1967.

ATTITUDES: PATIENT
  "The attempted suicide; true or false malady," by C. Z.
    Mieville. KRANKENPFL 64:432-435, December, 1971.

  "The chronic wrist-slasher," by Graff. HOSP TOP 45:61+,
    November, 1967.

  "Suicide: the patient's viewpoint," NT 61:1700, December
    10, 1965.

ATTITUDES: PREMEDITATION
  "Doctor reports on premeditated acts," NEW YORK TIMES
    43:1, November 17, 1957.

ATTITUDES: PREVENTION
  SEE PREVENTION

ATTITUDES: REASONS

ATTITUDES: REASONS
  SEE MOTIVATION

ATTITUDES: REACTIONS TO DEATH AND SUICIDE
  "Changing attitudes to death: a survey of contributions
    in Psychological Abstracts over a thirty year period,"
    by M. Williams. HUM REL 19:405-423, November, 1966.

  "Death anxiety in suicide attempters," by R. E. Tarter,
    et al. PSYCHOL REP 34:895-897, June, 1974.

  "Death ideation in suicidal patients," by S. Eisenthal.
    J ABNORM PSYCHOL 73:162-167, April, 1968.

  "Emotional reactions to death and suicide," by J. H.
    Massernan. AM PRACT & DIGEST TREAT (SUPP) 5:41-46,
    November, 1954.

  "Fear of death of suicidal persons," by D. Lester.
    PSYCHOL REP (SUPP) 20:1077-1078, June, 1967.

  "Some reflections on death and suicide," by E. S. Shneid-
    man. FOLIA PSYCHIAT NEUROL JAP 19:317-325, 1965.

ATTITUDES: RELIGION
  "A phenomenological approach to understanding suicidal
    behavior," by B. J. Stevens. J PSYCHIATR NURS 9:33-
    35, September-October, 1971.

  "Giving and taking one's life: case of N. R. Morrison,"
    CHRISTIAN CENT 82:1404, November 17, 1965; "discuss-
    ion," 83:84, January 19, 1966.

  "Phenomenological study of suicide notes," by J. Jacobs.
    SOC PROB 15:60-72, Summer, 1967.

ATTITUDES: RESEARCH
  SEE ALSO: RESEARCH
  "Suicide research shows facts versus fables," SCI N L
    80:384, December 9, 1961.

ATTITUDES: SOCIOLOGY
  "Comparative study of suicide," by W. L. Li. INT J
    COMP SOCIOL 12:281-286, December, 1971.

ATTITUDES: SOCIOLOGY

"Durkheim's concept of anomie and its relationship to divorce," by B. G. Cashion. SOCIOL & SOC RES 55: 72-81, October, 1970.

"Socio-structural analysis of murder, suicide, and economic crime in Ceylon," by A. L. Wood. AM SOCIOL R 26:744-753, October, 1961.

"Theory of status integration and its relationship to suicide," by J. P. Gibbs, et al. AM SOCIOL R 23:140-147, April, 1958.

ATTITUDES: SOLUTION
"A cry for help: suicide and accident proneness," by McGuire. J PSYCHIAT NURS 2:500+, September-October, 1964.

"TV Program shows suicide as possible solution to problem," NEW YORK TIMES 51:2, July 11, 1957.

ATTITUDES: THEORY
"Influence of suggestion on suicide: substantive and theoretical implications of the Werther Effect," by D. P. Phillips. AM SOCIOL R 39:340-354, June, 1974.

BEREAVEMENT
"Children's disturbed reactions to parent suicide," by A. C. Cain, et al. AM J ORTHOPSYCHIAT 36:873-880, October, 1966.

"Recent bereavement in relation to suicide," by J. Bunch. J PSYCHOSOM R 16:361-366, August, 1972.

BIBLIOGRAPHY: DYNAMICS
"The dynamics of suicide: a review of the literature," by L. Beall. BULL SUICIDOLOGY 1-16, March, 1969.

BIBLIOGRAPHY: GENERAL
"Bibliography and abstracts on suicide," BULL SUICIDOLOGY 1:19-32, July, 1967.

CANCER: SUICIDE AS ALTERNATIVE TO DEATH BY
"Doctor urges study of incidence of suicide as alternative to dying from cancer," NEW YORK TIMES 15:5, December, 1971.

CANCER: SUICIDE AS ALTERNATIVE TO DEATH BY

"I have cancer," by J. Harris.   NM 138:71-72, May 31,
   1974.

"Suicide among cancer patients," by P. Campbell.   CONN
   HEALTH BULL 80:207-212, 1966.

CHILDREN: ATTEMPTED SUICIDE
   SEE PARASUICIDE

CHILDREN: GENERAL
   SEE ALSO: PARASUICIDE: CHILDREN
   "Children and suicide," TIME 63:95, April 5, 1954.

"Death at an early age," by Ross. CA MENT HEALTH 18:7+,
   November-December, 1970.

"Suicide in children," by B. Y. O'Dell. PARENTS MAG 44:
   58-59+, January, 1969.

"Suicide in childhood and adolescence," by M. Clark.
   NEA J 58:32-33+, November, 1964.

"Suicide in children and adolescents," by Lampe.   J SCHL
   HEALTH 34:390+, October, 1964.

"Children in the dark," by M. Clark.   PTA MAG 55:10-13,
   May, 1961.

"Children who want to die," by Y. Horn. PTA MAG 68:18-
   21, November, 1973.

CHILDREN: GIRLS
   SEE ALSO ADOLESCENCE: GIRLS
   "Generation gap: girl kills herself instead of pet dog,"
   NEWSWEEK 71:32, February 19, 1968.

"Girls outnumber boys in suicide attempts," SCI N L 84:
   328, November 23, 1963.

"Tragedy of young girl suicides," by A. McMann. COSMO
   140:78-80, June, 1956.

CHILDREN: HANDICAPPED
   "Suicide attempt by a ten-year-old after quadruple
   amputations," by H. L. Resnik. JAMA 212:1211-1212,
   May 18, 1970.

CHILDREN: PREDICTION OF SUICIDAL TENDENCIES IN

CHILDREN: PREDICTION OF SUICIDAL TENDENCIES IN
  SEE PREDICTION

CHILDREN: PREVENTION OF SUICIDE IN
  SEE PREVENTION

CHILDREN: REACTIONS TO SUICIDE
  SEE ALSO: BEREAVEMENT
  "Children's disturbed reactions to parent suicide," by
  A. C. Cain, et al. AM J ORTHOPSYCH 36:873-880, Octo-
  ber, 1966.

CHILDREN: REASONS FOR SUICIDE BY
  SEE MOTIVATION

COLLEGE STUDENTS
  SEE STUDENTS: COLLEGE

COUNSELING
  SEE ALSO: PREVENTION
  "Counseling suicide survivors," by D. Schuyler.   NURS
  DIG 2:66-69, October, 1974.

  "Counseling the suicidal patient," by M. Frost.   NM
  139:74-75, July 5, 1974.

  "Survey of suicide counseling available to students in
  metropolitan Richmond," PUBLIC HEALTH REP (WASH) 84:
  118+, February, 1969.

CULTURAL DIFFERENCES: ADOLESCENTS
  "Adolescent suicide at an Indian reservation," by L. H.
  Dizmang, et al. AM J ORTHOPSYCH 44:43-49, January,
  1974.

  "Cultural factors in suicide of Japanese youth with
  focus on personality," by M. Iga.   SOC & SOC RES
  46:75-90, October, 1961.

  "Indian teenage suicides shock investigators,"   IMAGO
  12:11+, June, 1970.

CULTURAL DIFFERENCES: ADOLESCENTS

"Suicide, sex, and the discovery of the German adolescent," by S. Fishman. HIST.ED Q 10:170-188, Summer, 1970.

"Student suicides cause concern in England," SCI N L 75:185, March 21, 1959.

"Why are the suicides of young blacks increasing?" by R. H. Seiden. HSMHA HEALTH REP 87:3-8, January, 1972.

"Young love in Japan," TIME 65:32, January 17, 1955.

CULTURAL DIFFERENCES: AMERICAN INDIANS
"Adolescent suicide at an Indian reservation," by L. H. Dizmang, et al. AM J ORTHOPSYCH 44:43-49, January, 1974.

"Epidemiological study of suicide and attempted suicide among the Papago Indians," by R. D. Conrad, et al. AM J PSYCHIAT 131:69-72, January, 1974.

"The extent and significance of suicide among American Indians today," by R. J. Havighurst. MENT HYG 55: 174-177, April, 1971.

"Indian teenage suicides shock investigators," IMAGO 12:11+, June, 1970.

"New Indian war -- against suicide," by Bach. TODAY'S HEALTH 48:16+, October, 1970.

"Observations on suicidal behavior among American Indians," by H. L. Resnik, et al. AM J PSYCHIAT 127: 882-887, January, 1971.

"Suicide among the Cheyenne Indians," by L. H. Dizmang. BULL SUICIDOL 8-11, July, 1967.

"Suicide attempt patterns among the Navajo Indians," by S. I. Miller, et al. INT J SOC PSYCHIAT 17:189-193, Summer, 1971.

CULTURAL DIFFERENCES: BLACKS

CULTURAL DIFFERENCES: BLACKS
   "Black suicide," by L. Banks. EBONY 25:76-78+, May, 1970.

   "Black suicide," by H. Hendin. TRANS-ACTION 7:85+, July,
   1970. "Review," by W. L. Yancey. 7:85+, July, 1970.

   "Racial oppression and black suicide: excerpts for Black
   Suicide," by H. Hendin. CUR 114:29-36, January, 1970.

   "Search for prevention of black suicides," US NEWS 77:
   47-48, July 1, 1974.

   "Suicide: growing menace to black women," by J. Slater.
   EBONY 28:152-154+, September, 1973.

   "Why Negro suicides are increasing," by J. N. Woodford.
   EBONY 20:89-90+, July, 1965.

CULTURAL DIFFERENCES: ESKIMOS
   "Notes on Eskimo patterns of suicide," by A. H. Leighton, et al. S W J ANTHROP 11:327-338, Winter, 1955.

CULTURAL DIFFERENCES: GENERAL
   SEE ALSO: OTHER COUNTRIES
   "Focus on suicide: self-destruction still a puzzle to
   scientists despite research: suicide rate varies widely
   by nationality, race, sex; prevention centers spread,"
   by H. G. Lawson. WALL ST J 162:1+, September 20, 1963.

   "Fusion and frustration: dimensions in the cross-cultural ethnopsychology of suicide," by A. E. Hippler.
   AM ANTHROP 71:1085-1087, December, 1969.

CULTURAL DIFFERENCES: HAWAII
   "Suicide: an ethnic comparison in Hawaii," by R. A. Kal-
   ish. BULL SUICIDOL 37-43, December, 1968.

DRUGS: ACCIDENTAL POISONING
   "Survey on suicides and accidental poisoning," by J.
   Baker. NT 67:258-261, March 4, 1971.

DRUGS: CARE AND TREATMENT
   "Caring for the drug-poisoned patient," by Horgan. RN
   25:62+, June, 1962.

DRUGS: CARE AND TREATMENT

"Narcosis therapy," by K. Moreton. NM 134:41-43, April 7, 1972.

"Suicide by poisoning. Reception and treatment in causality," by Skellern. NT 61:1011+, July 23, 1965.

"Sucide by poisoning. Suicide and the survivor," by Kessel. NT 61:960+, July 16, 1965.

DRUGS: GENERAL
"Poisoning by drugs," by H. Helwig. DEUTSCH ZBL KRANKENPFL 11:65-67, February, 1967.

"Self-poisoning," by R. Goulding. NM 133:13-14, December 3, 1971.

"Suicides, drugs and the open hospital," by Krieger. HOSP TOP 45:23+, July, 1967.

DRUGS: OVERDOSE
"Drug overdose," by L. Brown, et al. NURS J 69:8-17, July, 1971.

"Drug overdoses in a Canadian city," by M. Sims, et al. AM J PUB HEALTH 63:215-226, March, 1973.

"Overdose," by Nemo. NT 68:1040+, August 17, 1973.

"Suicide in drug users?" by M. Huizer. TIJDSCHR ZIEKENVERPL 27:163-164, February 19, 1974.

DRUGS: PREVENTION OF SUICIDE BY
"Doctors can help prevent suicides by poisoning," SCI N L 73:338, May 31, 1958.

DRUGS: SLEEPING PILLS
"An overdose of sleep," EMERG MED 2:78+, September, 1970.

"Sleeping pills popular for committing suicide," SCI N L 80:368, December 2, 1961.

DRUGS: TRANQUILIZERS
"Tranquilizers as suicide pills," NEW YORK TIMES 15:7, August 10, 1963.

ECONOMICS

ECONOMICS
  SEE MOTIVATION

EDUCATION: ACHIEVEMENT
  "Suicide and educational attainment in a transitional
    society," by W. L. Li. SOCIOL Q 13:252-258, Spring,
    1972.

  "Suicide rate greater for more educated," NEW YORK TIMES
    19:3, March 18, 1951.

EDUCATION: GENERAL
  "Education for death: health education at the University
    of Maryland," by D. Leviton. JOHPER 40:46-47+, Spring,
    1969.

  "The educational play," by B. B. Bauer. J CON ED NURS
    2:46-48, November-December, 1971.

  "The need for education on death and suicide," by D.
    Leviton. J SCH HEALTH 39:270-274, April, 1969.

  "Suicidal ignorance re: suicide," SCI DIG 72:55, Aug-
    ust, 1972.

  "Will we ever learn?" NT 68:983, August 10, 1972.

EDUCATION: STUDENTS
  SEE STUDENTS

EDUCATION: TEACHER
  "Death of a teacher," NEWSWEEK 51:72, February 10, 1958.

ETHICS
  "Biological revolution's ethical problems debated," AJN
    72:627+, April, 1972.

  "Ethics of suicide," by T. S. Szasz. ANTIOCH R 31:7-17,
    Spring, 1971.

  "Moral and financial limitations of therapy," by M.
    Conte, et al. SEM THER 44:145-147, March, 1968.

ETHNIC
  SEE: OTHER COUNTRIES, OTHER CULTURES

GERIATRICS: GENERAL

GERIATRICS: GENERAL
"Attempted suicide in old age," by I. R. Batchelor, et
al. BRIT MED J 2:1186-1190, November 28, 1953.

"Attempted suicide in the aged," by J. W. Hickman. J
IND MED ASS 58:1138-1140, October, 1965.

"Depression and suicide in the geriatric patient," by
K. Wolff. J AM GERIAT SOC 17:668-672, July, 1969.

"Psychiatric study of attempted suicide in persons over
60 years of age," by P. O'Neal, et al. AMA ARCH NEUR
& PSYCHIAT 75:275-284, March, 1956.

"Suicide and aging," by H. L. Resnik, et al. J AM GERIAT
SOC 18:152-158, February, 1970.

"Suicide in later life," by P. Sainsbury. GERONT CLIN
4:161-170, 1962.

"Suicide in old age," by P. Sainsbury. PROC ROY SOC MED
54:266-268, April, 1961.

"Suicide in the aged," by A. W. Deibel. J PSYCHIAT
NURS 9:39, May-June, 1971.

"Suicide in the aged," by F. B. Gage. AJN 71:2153-2155,
November, 1971.

GERIATRICS: MALE SUICIDES
"Bad times drive more old men than young to suicide,"
SCI N L 57:377, June 17, 1950.

GERIATRICS: NURSING CARE
"Is your elderly patient talking about suicide?,"
by R.L. Garrard. CONSULTANT 13:49-50, January, 1973.

GERIATRICS: RATE
"Older persons may cause increase in suicide rate,"
SCI N L 77:280, April 30, 1960.

GERIATRICS: STATISTICS
"Suicide among older people," (U.S., 1918-1949),
METROPOLITAN LIFE INS CO STATIS BUL p.9-10,
May, 1950.

GERIATRICS: WIDOWHOOD
"Suicide among the elderly: isolating widowhood and
and mitigating alternatives," by E.W. Bock, et al.
J MARRIAGE & FAM 34:24-31, February, 1972.

GROUP SUICIDE
"The suicide six: observations on suicidal behavior
and group function," by D. Reiss. INT J SOC
PSYCHIAT 14:201-12, Summer, 1968.

HISTORICAL
"Discussion of suicide in the eighteenth century,"
by L.G. Crocker. J HIST IDEAS 13:47-72, January, 1952.

HOMICIDE: CITIES
"Indices of suicide and homicide by states and
cities: some southern-non-southern contrasts with
implications for research," by A. L. Porterfield.
AM SOCIOL R 14: 481-90, August, 1949.

HOMICIDE: ECONOMIC DEVELOPMENT
"Suicide, homicide, and economic development," by
R. Quinney. SOC FORCES 43:401-6, March, 1965.

HOMICIDE: GENERAL
"Suicides and homicides," by H. Alpert. AM SOCIOL R
15:673, October, 1950.

"Suicide and homicide," by A.F. Henry, et al. "Review,"
by A. Beegle. RURAL SOCIOL 20:68, March, 1955.

HOMICIDE: MULTIPLE MURDER
"Burkean analysis of the rhetorical dimensions of
a multiple murder and suicide," by J.Y. Fisher.
"Reply with rejoinder," by P.G. Burgess. Q J
SPEECH 60:175-89, 60:225-34, April, 1974.

HOMICIDE: SOCIOLOGY
"Suicide, homicide, and the socialization of ag-
gression," by M. Gold. AM J SOCIOL 63:651-61,
May, 1958.

HOMICIDE: SOCIOLOGY & COUNTRIES
"Suicide, homicide, and social structure in Ceylon,"
by J.H. Straus, et al. AM J SOCIOL 58:461-9,
March, 1953.

HOMICIDE: TRAFFIC
  "Traffic fatalities, suicide, and homicide," by
    A. L. Porterfield. AM SOCIOL R 25:897-901,
    December, 1960.

HOSPITAL: DETECTION OF SUICIDAL PATIENT
  "Detection and management of the suicidal patient,"
    by Mintz. DM p.3+, July, 1961.

HOSPITAL: HEALTH SERVICES
  "Emergency mental health services in a general
    hospital," by Beahan. HOSP & COMM PSYCHIAT
    21:81+, March, 1970.

HOSPITAL: ROLE
  "Hospital's duty to the suicidal," BR MED J 4:754,
    December 19, 1970.

  "The hospital's obligation toward suicide-prone
    patients," by Litman. HOSPITALS 40:64+, Decem-
    ber 16, 1966.

HOSPITAL: SUICIDES-GENERAL
  "Suicides, drugs, and the open hospital," by
    Krieger. HOSP & COMM PSYCHIAT 17:196+, July, 1966.

  "Suicides, drugs, and the open hospital," by
    Krieger. HOSP TOPICS 45:23+, July, 1967.

  "Suicide in the hospital," by Davidson. HOSPITALS
    43:55+, November 16, 1969.

HOSPITAL: PATIENTS
  "Management of the attempted suicide patient:
    indications for psychiatric hospitalization," by
    O.S. Surman , et al. MED INSIGHT 4:14-21, July, 1972.

  "Suicide among general medical and surgical hospi-
    tal patients with malignant neoplasms," by N.
    Farberow , et al. VET ADM MED BULL 9:1-11, 1963.

HOSPITAL: PATIENT-GENERAL
  "Morphinist: incident at Hospital of the City of
    Vienna, 1928," by R. Berczeller. NEW YORKER
    42:141-2+, April 16, 1966.

HOSPITAL: PATIENT -- GENERAL

"The suicidal patient in the general ward," by
Sawyer. N 58:1587+, December 14, 1962.

"Suicidal patients," by H. S. Greer. NURS MIRROR
130:36-37, January 16, 1970.

HOSPITAL: PATIENT -- PREVENTION
SEE ALSO PREVENTION
"Suicide in hospitalized patients: clues and pre-
vention," by Bennett, et al. HOSP MED 1:36+,
February, 1965.

"Suicide prevention: the hospital's role," by
Shneidman. HOSP PRACTICE 3:56+, September, 1968.

HOSPITAL: POISONING
SEE ALSO DRUGS
"Medicosocial problems in acute self-induced
poisoning," by N. Schnirer. REV INFIRM 22:533-
537, June, 1972.

HOSPITAL: PSYCHOLOGICAL
SEE ALSO MENTAL PATIENTS
"The psychological autopsy: a technique for in-
vestigating a hospital suicide," by K. Neill, et al.
HOSP COMM PSYCHIAT 25:33-36, January, 1974.

"Effects of a suicide in a psychiatric hospital,"
by L. Kayton. ARCH GEN PSYCHIAT (CHICAGO)
17: 187-194, August, 1967.

IMMOLATION: SPECIFIC PERSONS
"In witness to man's oneness: concerning self-
immolations of N. Morrison and R. LaPorte," by
B. Reynolds. CHRISTIAN CENT 83:81, January 19, 1966.

IMMOLATION: VIETNAM
"End of the glow: new suicides in Saigon," TIME
82:32, December 13, 1963.

"Fiery rebellion: self-immolations in South Vietnam,"
NEWSWEEK 67:48-49, June 13, 1966.

"His canon against self-slaughter: spies and self-
destruction," AMERICA 103:371, June 18, 1960.

IMMOLATION: VIETNAM

"Immolations and consensus: justification of innocence,"
   by A. Towne. CHR CENT 83:72-75, January 19, 1966.

"Light that failed: self-immolation in Vietnam,"
   TIME 87:39, June 10, 1966.

"Reluctant way: self-immolation in Vietnam," by
   M. Hope. ANTIOCH R 27:149-163, Summer, 1967.

INDIVIDUAL: GENERAL
"Werther effect: following the famous suicides:
   research by D. Phillips," by G. Gregg. PSYCHOL
   TODAY 8:28+, October, 1974.

INDIVIDUAL: IMMIGRANT
"Rate of immigrant suicide," WORLD FED FOR MENTAL
   HEALTH NEW YORK TIMES 31:3, September 3, 1952.

INDIVIDUAL: SPECIFIC PERSONS
"Acting out -- The story of Doris," by Crang NT
   66:1495+, November 19, 1970.

"Aftermath: death of N. Nakasa," by R. Jenkins.
   ESQUIRE 65:16+, June, 1966.

"Case study of Geraldine," by C. Flowers. NURS
   MIRROR 130:33-5, May 8, 1970.

"Easter gift for Tommy," by Sullivan. RN 26:69+,
   April, 1963.

"From euphoria to suicide: death of E.A. Brudno,"
   TIME 101:67, June 18, 1973.

"Giving and taking one's life: case of N.R. Morrison,"
   CHRISTIAN CENT 82:1404, November 17,1965; "Discussion," CHRISTIAN CENT 83:84, January 19, 1966.

"In witness to man's oneness: concerning self-
   immolations of N. Morrison and R. LaPorte," by
   B. Reynolds. CHRISTIAN CENT 83:81, January 19, 1966.

"Judy and I," by Branscum. J PSYCHIAT NURS 3:433+,
   September-October, 1965.

INDIVIDUAL: SPECIFIC PERSONS

"Man in the middle: suicide of P.L. Cabell of Beecher
High School, Flint, Michigan," by L. Wainwright.
LIFE 73:55-6+, July 21,1972.

"Nursing care study: Laura--recovery from an overdose," by A. Townsend. NURS TIMES 69:1446-8,
November 1, 1973.

"Peace suicides: Joan Fox and Craig Badiall of
Blackwood, N.J.," by E. Asinof. SEVENTEEN 29:174+,
March, 1970.

"Suicide in hospitalized patients: clues and prevention," by Bennett,et al. HOSP MED 1:36+,
February, 1965.

"Sylvia Plath reconsidered," by J. Romano. COMMEN-
TARY 57:47-52, April, 1974.

"Tragedy at Beecher High: P.L. Cabell's suicide," by
A.E. Smith EBONY 27:154-6+, October, 1972.

"Ultimate Goldberg: death of Russell Aubrey Penning-
ton," NEWSWEEK 66:30-1, July 12, 1965.

"What killed Bob Lyons? Executive's emotional problems," by H. Levinson. HARVARD BSNS R 41:127-42+,
January, 1963.

INDIVIDUAL: TYPE OF PERSON
"Suicide: the kind of person who may try it," by
L. Alexander. RN 29:33-42, March, 1966.

LAW: CRIME
"Crime of suicide," ECONOMIST 196:871-2, September 3,
1960.

"Should suicide be called a crime? English law,"
CHRISTIAN CENT 77:1078, September 21, 1960.

LAW: CRIME-STATE-COUNTRY
"Is suicide a crime in North Carolina?" by M.
Warren. POPULAR GOVT 37:12-16, June, 1971.

"British Commons urges repeal of suicide as crime,"
NEW YORK TIMES 5:5, March 1, 1958.

LAW: GENERAL
"Legal condonement of unintentional suicide," IND MED
28:46-48, January, 1959; "Discussion," by M. A.
Wolf. IND MED 28:252, May, 1959.

"Medical, social, and legal aspects of suicide," by
R. Dripps, et al. JAMA 171:523-527, October 3, 1959.

LAW: INTERPRETATION
"The judicial interpretation of suicide," UNIV PA LAW
R 105:391-410, January, 1957.

"Suicide and the law," by K. Robinson. SPEC 200:317,
March 14, 1958.

LAW: POLICE
"Police aspects of suicide: legal aspects of suicide,
handling suicidal persons; suicide prevention services," by R. E. Litman. POLICE 10:14-18, January-
February, 1966.

LAW: RIGHTS
"Freedom to choose one's death," by J. Meerloo. NATION
200:314-315, March 29, 1965.

"Law and christial morals in the liberal society:
should suicide be a crime?" by N. St. John-Stevas.
DUBLIN R 234:20, Spring, 1960.

"Now, a right to suicide?" by R. Boeth. NEWSWEEK 82:
78+, October 29, 1973.

"Suicide and civil rights," by A. J. Snider. SCI DIG
67:54, January, 1970.

"Suicide and suicide prevention: a legal analysis,"
by R. E. Schulman. AM BAR ASS J 54:855-862, September, 1968.

LITERATURE
"Alejandro Casona and suicide," by C. H. Leighton.
HISPANIA 55:436-445, September, 1972.

"Confucius and suicide," TIME 73:58, January 26, 1959.

"Comment on Faber's analysis of Jocastra's suicide in Oedipus Rex," by D. Lester. PSYCHOL REP 34:182, February, 1974.

"Donne and Charron," by R. G. Collmer. ENG STUD 46: 482-488, December, 1965.

"Extremists of Al Alvarez (review article)," by G. Grigson. ENCOUNTER 89:59-60, August, 1972.

"Hamlet's to be or not to be soliloquy: once more unto the breach," by V. F. Petronella. STUD PHILOL 71: 72-88, January, 1974.

"Howell's Maggie," by D. Aaron. NEW ENG Q 38:85-90, March, 1965.

"Impotence and self-destruction in The Country Wife," by W. Freedman. ENG STUD 53:421-431, October, 1972.

"J. D. Salinger: suicide and survival in the modern world," by T. L. Gross. S ATLAN Q 68:454-462, Autumn, 1969.

"John Whiting and the theme of self-destruction," by J. D. Hurrell. MOD DRAMA 8:134-141, September, 1965.

"Liberation in suicide: Mersault in the light of Dante," by R. Pickens, et al. FRENCH R 41:524-531, February, 1968.

"Lily Bart and the beautiful death," by C. G. Wolff. AM LIT 46:16-40, March, 1974.

"Menoeceus in the Thebaid of Statius," by D. W. Vessey. CLASS PHILOL 66:236-243, Octo-er, 1971.

"Plato, Phaedo, 62," by A. L. Taran. AM J PHILOL 87: 326-336, July, 1966.

"Pope's Elegy to the memory of an unfortunate lady," by H. D. Weinbrot. MOD LANG Q 32:255-267, September, 1971.

"Racine and the problem of suicide," by M. Monaco. PMLA 70:441-454, June, 1955.

LITERATURE

"Return of the Native: Hardy's map and Eustacia's
suicide," by K. Zenefrow. 19TH CENT FICT 28:214-220,
September, 1973.

"Salinger's Seymour's suicide," by J. E. Bryan. COL ENG
24:226-229, December, 1962. "Reply with rejoinder,"
by W. French. COL ENG 24:563-564, April, 1963.

"Self-destruction in Oedipus Rex," by M. D. Faber. AM
IMAGO 27:41-51, Spring, 1970.

"Study of literary reactions to suicide-impulse," by W.
Sheed. NEW YORK TIMES 7:2, May 7, 1972.

"Suicide and Brutus' philosophy in Julius Caesar," by
M. Sacharoff. J HIST IDEAS 33:115-122, January, 1972.

"Suicide and sacrifice in Tolstoy's Ethics," by G. W.
Spence. RUSS R 22:157-167, April, 1963.

"Sylvia Plath reconsidered," by J. Romano. COMMENTARY
57:47-52, April, 1974.

"Werther effect: following the famous suicides: research
by D. Phillips," by G. Gregg. PSYCHOL TODAY 8:28+,
October, 1974.

MEANING OF DEATH
"Crypto-suicide," by J. Donnelly. MED INSIGHT 5:24-27+,
September, 1973.

"Meaningful death," by J. C. Evans. CHR CENT 82:1598,
December 29, 1965.

MENTAL PATIENTS
SEE ALSO: PSYCHIATRY
"Attempt to employ a sentence completion test for the
detection of psychiatric patients with suicidal ideas,"
by H. Y. Efron. J CONSULT PSYCHOL 24:156-160, April,
1960.

"Attempted suicides admitted to the mental health department. Victoria, Australia: a socio-epidemiological
study," by J. Krupinski, et al. INT J SOC PSYCHIAT
13:5-13, Winter, 1966.

"A behavioral approach to irrational anxiety and insom-
nia," by M. C. Maultsby, Jr. J AM MED WOM ASS 27:416-
419, August, 1972.

"Broken homes among attempted suicides and psychiatric
out-patients: a comparative study," by J. G. Bruhn.
J MENT SCI 108:772-779, November, 1962.

"By psychotics (in psychiatric hospitals)," by D. M.
Banen. J NERV & MENT DIS 120:349-357, November-
December, 1954.

"Case history and hospitalization factors in suicides
of neuropsychiatric hospital patients," by N. L. Farberow, et al. J NERV MENT DIS 142:32-44, January, 1966.

"The communication of suicidal intent prior to psychiatric hospitalization: a study of 87 patients," by W. B.
Delong, et al. AM J PSYCHIAT 117:695-705, February,
1961.

"Community growth, depressive disorders, and suicide,"
by H. Wechsler. AM J SOCIOL 67:9-16, July, 1961.

"Comparative study of attempted suicides and psychiatric
out-patients," by J. G. Bruhn. BRIT J PREV SOC MED
17:197-201, October, 1963.

"Coping with psychiatric emergencies," by L. Robinson.
NURSING (Jenkintown) 3:42-44, July, 1973.

"Cross-validation of a Rorschach checklist associated
with suicidal tendencies," by I. B. Weiner. J CONSULT
PSYCHOL 25:312-315, August, 1961.

"Culture and mental disorders: a study of attempted
suicide," by E. Robins, et al. HUM ORGAN 16:7-11,
Winter, 1958.

"Depression, despair, and suicide," by E. Maycock. TIMES
ED SUPP 2647:407, February 11, 1966.

"Disaster during psychiatric treatment. An intrapsych-
ic problem for the physician," by L. W. Woods. CAN
PSYCHIATR ASS J 18:67-70, February, 1973.

"Double suicide in psychiatric hospital patients,"
   by J.P. Crawford, et al. BRIT J PSYCHIAT 112:
   1231-5, December, 1966.

"Dyadic crisis suicides in mental hospital patients,"
   by N. L. Farberow, et al. J ABNORM PSYCHOL 78:
   77-85, August, 1971.

"Effects of a suicide in a psychiatric hospital,"
   by L. Kayton, et al. ARCH GEN PSYCHIAT (Chicago)
   17:187-94, August, 1967.

"Effects of two simultaneous cognitive and affective
   stimuli on a group of chronic schizophrenic patients
   with suicidal ideation," by E. Starer. J CLIN
   PSYCHOL 16:341-3, July, 1960.

"Follow-up of neuropsychiatric patients in suicide
   observation status," by S. Eisenthal, et al.
   PUBLIC HEALTH REP 81:977-90, November, 1965.

"In state hospital for mentally ill," by S. Levy,
   et al. J NERV & MENT DIS 117:504-14, June, 1954.

"Investigation of certain psychodiagnostic indica-
   tions of suicidal tendencies and depression in
   mental hospital patients (with special regard to
   Rorschach test)," by D. C. Broida. PSYCHIAT
   QUART 28:453-464, July, 1954.

"Item differentiation analysis of MMPIS of suicidal
   neuropsychiatric patients," by N. L. Farberow,
   et al. PSYCHOL REP 20:607-17, April, 1967.

"Management of depression and suicide attempts,"
   by C. H. Branch. NORTHWEST MED 65:1060-4,
   December, 1966.

"Mental illness and suicide," by R. W. Parnell
   TIMES ED SUP 1979:303, April 3, 1953.

"Montly patterns of suicide and mental illness,"
   by D. E. Sanborn, et al. DIS NERV SYST 30:551-2,
   August, 1969.

"Moon phases and mental hospital admissions," by
A. D. Pokorny. J PSYCHIAT NURS 6:325-7, November-
December, 1968.

"Prediction of suicide in a psychiatric hospital,"
by R. A. Dean, et al. J CLIN PSYCHOL 23:296-301,
July, 1967.

"Predictive value of the 'scale for assessing suicide
risk' (SASR) with hospitalized psychiatric patients,"
by J. H. Resnick, et al. J CLIN PSYCHOL 29:187-
90, April, 1973.

"Psychiatric consultations in a general hospital,"
by T. R. Kearney. BRIT J PSYCHIAT 112:1237-40,
December, 1966.

"Psychiatric emergencies," by K. E. Rogerson. NURS
CLIN NORTH AM 8:457-66, September, 1973.

"Psychiatric evaluation of 100 cases of suicidal
attempts in Shiraz, Iran," by H. Gharagozlu-
Hamadani. INT J SOC PSYCHIATRY 18:140-4, Summer,
1972.

"Psychiatrist examines suicide," by Friedman.
TODAY'S HLTH 41:56+, December, 1963.

"Psychiatry and suicide: the management of a mistake," by D. W. Light,Jr. AM J SOCIOL 77:821-38,
March, 1972.

"Psychopathic disorder treated in a hospital for
the mentally subnormal," by Suokas. NM 128:17+,
May 30, 1969.

"Psychotherapeutic approach to the suicidal
patient," by D. Y. Mayer. BR J PSYCHIAT 119:629-
33, December, 1971.

"Psychotherapy and the danger of suicide," AMER
J PSYCHOTHER 15:181-3, April, 1961.

"Psychotherapy of the hospitalized suicidal patient,"
by A. A. Stone, et al. AMER J PSYCHOTHER 22:
15-25, January, 1968.

"Psychotherapy of the suicidal patient," by R. S. Mintz. AMER J PSYCHOTHER 15:348-67, July, 1961.

"Psychotherapy of suicidal patient," by L. M. Moss. NY J MED 66:3020-3, December 1, 1966.

"Recognition of emotional disturbance and the prevention of suicide," by A. Capstick. BRIT MED J 5180:1179-82, April 16, 1960.

"Relationship between obsessions and suicidal attempts in depressive psychosis," by N. L. Gittleson. BRIT J PSYCHIAT 112:889-90, September, 1966.

"Relationship of mental disorder to suicidal behavior. Review of recent issues," by D. Lester. NY STATE J MED 71:1503-5, June 15, 1971.

"Role of psychotherapy in the treatment of suicidal persons. On the deromanticization of death," by E. S. Shneidman. AM J PSYCHOTHER 25:4-17, January, 1971.

"Self-evaluation of suicidal mental hospital patients," by D. K. Kamano, et al. J CLIN PSYCHOL 22:278-9, July, 1966.

"72-hour psychiatric detention. Clinical observation and treatment in a county general hospital," by J. A. Guido, et al. ARCH GEN PSYCHIAT (Chicago) 16:233-8, February, 1967.

"Six aspects of mental illness. Suicide and attempted suicide. Part 2," by Nixon, et al. NM 119:407+, January 29, 1965.

"Social structure and the ecological distribution of mental illness, suicide, and delinquency," by C. Bagley, et al. PSYCHOL MED 3:177-87, May, 1973.

"Some aspects of suicide in psychiatric patients in Southend," by A. A. Robin, et al. BRIT J PSYCHIAT 114:739-47, June, 1968.

"Some considerations on the treatment of suicidal
depressive patients," by P. Friedman. AMER J
PSYCHOTHER 16:379-86, July, 1962.

"Some psychiatric non-sequelae of childhood bereavement," by O. Hill. BRIT J PSYCHIAT 116:
679-80, June, 1970.

"Some psychological features of persons who have
attempted suicide," by A. E. Philip, et al.
BRIT J PSYCHIAT 114:1299-300, October, 1968.

"Study of psychiatric emergencies. Suicide," by
C. H. Browning, et al. PSYCHIATRY MED 1:359-66,
October, 1970.

"Study of suicidal attempts in patients admitted to
a state psychiatric hospital," by J. E. Oltman,
et al. DIS NERV SYST 23:433-9, August, 1962.

"Study of suicides in a mental hospital," by A.
R. Beisser, et al. DIS NERV SYST 22:365-9,
July, 1961.

"Suicidal behavior, sex, and mental disorder," by
D. Lester. PSYCHOL REP 27:61-2, August, 1970.

"Suicidal behavior: an attempt to modify the environment," by N. Lukianowicz. BR J PSYCHIATRY
121:387-90, October, 1972.

"Suicidal solution as a function of ego-closeness-
ego-distance," by H. M. Voth, et al. ARCH GEN
PSYCHIAT (Chicago) 21:536-45, November, 1969.

"Suicide among patients in mental hospitals. A
study of the psychiatrists who conducted their
psychotherapy," by M. J. Kahne. PSYCHIATRY 31:
32-43, February, 1968.

"Suicide and natural death in a state hospital
population: a comparison of admission complaints,
MMPI profiles, and social competence factors," by
M. R. Ravensborg, et al. J CONSULT CLIN PSYCHOL
33:466-71, August, 1969.

"Suicide attempts and threats as goal-directed communications in psychotic males," by P. Kangas, et al. PSYCHOL REP 27:795-801, December, 1970.

"Suicide clues in psychotic patients," by R. G. Singer, et al. MENT HY 53:346-50, July, 1969.

"Suicide during psychiatric hospitalization," by R. F. Chapman. BULL MENNINGER CLIN 29:35-44, March, 1965.

"Suicide in mental hospital patients," by I. W. Sletten, et al. DIS NERV SYST 33:328-34, May, 1972.

"Suicide in schizophrenia," by N. P. Anderson. PERSPECT PSYCHIATR CARE 11:106-12, July-September, 1973.

"Suicides in schizophrenics," by H. Warnes. DIS NERV SYST 29:Suppl:35-40, May, 1968.

"Suicide precipitated by psychotherapy. A clinical contribution," by A. A. Stone. AM J PSYCHOTHER 25:18-26, January, 1971.

"Suicide prevention center in a public mental hospital," by H. H. Brunt, Jr., et al. MENT HY 52: 254-62, April, 1968.

"Suicide prevention on psychiatric wards," by A. E. Bennett, et al. MENT HOSP 16:105-8, March, 1965.

"Suicide clues in psychotic patients," by R. G. Singer, et al. MENT HYG 53:346-50, July, 1969.

"Suicide rates among current and former mental institution patients," by A. Temoche, et al. J NERV MENT DIS 138:124-30, February, 1964.

"Suicide rates in various psychiatric disorders," by A. D. Pokorny. J NERV MENT DIS 139:499-506, December, 1964.

MENTAL PATIENTS

"Suicide research: a critical review of strategies and
potentialities in mental hospitals," by M. J. Kahne.
INT J SOC PSYCHIAT 12:177-186, Summer, 1966.

"Suicides in mental hospitals: a study of the effects
of personnel and patient turnover," by M. J. Kahne.
J HEALTH SOC BEHAV 9:255-266, September, 1968.

"Survey of suicide among patients on home leave from a
mental hospital," by R. K. Bolin, et al. PSYCHIAT Q
42:81-89, 1968.

"Treatment of depression," by M. Hardial. NT 69:741-
743, June 7, 1973.

"Treatment of depression in relation to suicidal attempts,"
by A. Nomura. DIS NERV SYST 21:701-703, December, 1960.

MILITARY

"An analysis of suicide at a training center," by V.
Bloom. AM J PSYCHIAT 123:918-925, February, 1967.

"An incidence study of military personnel engaging in
suicidal behavior," by J. B. Sawyer. MILIT MED 134:
1440-1444, November, 1969.

"Incidents in military personnel," by H. Pozner. BRIT
J M PSYCHOL 26:93-109, 1953.

"The significance of the suicide gesture in the military,"
by G. J. Tucker, et al. AM J PSYCHIAT 123:854-861, January, 1967.

"A study of suicidal behavior in the military setting,"
by H. E. Russell, et al. MILIT MED 136:549-552, June,
1971.

"Suicidal gesture: study of 114 military patients hospitalized because of abortive suicide attempts," by
M. Fisch. AM J PSYCHIAT 111:33-36, July, 1954.

"Suicidal population of a military psychiatric center.
A review of ten years," by T. B. Hauschild. MILIT
MED 133:425-436, June, 1968.

MILITARY

"Suicidal reaction in the service environment," by A.
R. Mitchell. J ROY ARMY MED CORPS 109:215-219, 1963.

"Suicide by air force personnel 1958 to 1964," by P. F.
Eggertsen, et al. MILIT MED 133:26-32, January, 1968.

"Suicide in released prisoners of war," by D. Lester.
JAMA 225:747, August 13, 1973.

"Suicide in war veterans: rates and methods," by A. D.
Pokorny. J NERV MENT DIS 144:224-229, March, 1967.

"Suicide prevention in the military," by M. Rosenbaum,
et al. MILIT MED 135:500-501, June, 1970.

"Suicides and attempted suicides in the Norwegian Armed
Forces during peace time," by J. C. Englespad. MILIT
MED 133:437-448, June, 1968.

MOTIVATION: AGGRESSION
"Bullying one reason for girl's death: Southampton
report," TIMES ED SUPP 3064:6-7, February 15, 1974.

"Choosing to die: the decline of aggression and the rise
of suicide," by J. Binstock. FUTURIST 8:68-71, April,
1974.

"Suicide and aggression," by S. Eisenthal. PSYCHOL REP
21:45-51, December, 1967.

"Suicide as an aggressive act," by D. Lester. J PSYCHOL
66:47-50, May, 1967.

"Suicide as an aggressive act" a replication with a control for neuroticism," by D. Lester. J GEN PSYCHOL
79:83-86, July, 1968.

MOTIVATION: ALCOHOLISM
"Alcoholism and suicide," MED J AUST 1:620-621, March
20, 1971.

"Attempted suicide and alcoholism," by K. M. Koller, et
al. MED J AUST 2:835-837, November 9, 1968.

MOTIVATION: ALCOHOLISM

"Notes on the association between alcoholism and suicide,"
by P. C. Whitehead. INT J ADDICT 7:525-532, 1972.

"Prevalence of alcoholism in population and among suicides
and accidents from poisoning, Massachusetts 1938-1948,"
by J. Ipsen, Jr., et al. Q J STUD ALCOHOL 13:204-214,
June, 1952.

"Suicidal behavior during alcoholic blackouts," by J.
R. Morrison, et al. Q J STUD ALCOHOL 35, No. 2A:657-
659, June, 1974.

"Suicidal intent, alcoholism, and syndrome-related concepts," by F. Cutter, et al. Q J STUD ALCOHOL 31:861-
867, December, 1970.

"Suicide amongst alcoholics," by E. B. Ritson. BR J MED
PSYCHOL 41:235-242, September, 1968.

"Suicide and the interaction of alcoholism (liver cirr-
hosis) with the social situation,: by W. A. Rushing.
Q J STUD ALCOHOL 30:93-103, March, 1969.

"Suicide in alcoholics," by N. Kessel, et al. BR MED J
5268:1671-1672, December 23, 1961.

MOTIVATION: BEREAVEMENT
"Recent bereavement in relation to suicide," by J. Bunch.
J PSYCHOSOM RES 16:361-366, August, 1972.

MOTIVATION: BIRTHDATE
"Completed suicide and month of birth," by D. Lester,
et al. PSYCHOL REP 27:210, August, 1970.

MOTIVATION: BODY DONATION
"Body donation and suicide. Is there a relationship?"
by T. A. Flanagan, et al. ARCH GEN PSYCHIAT 28:732-
734, May, 1973.

MOTIVATION: CATHARSIS
"Suicide as catharsis," by R. G. Austin. LANCET 2:757,
October 7, 1972.

MOTIVATION: CLIMATE

MOTIVATION: CLIMATE
"Suicides and climatology," by E. Digon, et al. ARCH
ENVIRON HEALTH 12:279-286, March, 1966

MOTIVATION: COMMUNICATION
"Suicidal communication by adolescents. Study of two
matched groups of 60 teenagers," by E. K. Stevenson,
et al. DIS NERV SYST 33:112-122, February, 1972.

"Suicide and the communication of rage: a cross-cultural case study," by F. D. McCandless. AM J PSYCHIAT
125:197-205, August, 1968.

"Suicide as a message," by K. W. Berblinger. PSYCHO-
SOMATICS 5:144-146, May-June, 1964.

MOTIVATION: COMMUNITY
"Community growth, depressive disorders, and suicide,"
by H. Wechsler. AM J SOCIOL 67:9-16, July, 1961.

"Incidence of suicidal attempts in an urban community,"
by D. Parkin, et al. BR MED J 5454:133-138, July 17,
1965.

"Urban and rural suicide," by A. Capstick. J MENT SCI
106:1327-1336, October, 1960.

MOTIVATION: DEPRESSION -- GENERAL
"Apparent remissions in depressed suicidal patients,"
by S. Lesse. J NERV MENT DIS 144:291-296, April,
1967.

"Basic considerations in the psychotherapy of the depressed suicidal patient," by R. S. Mintz. AM J PSYCH-
OTHER 25:56-73, January, 1971.

"Depression," by H. Miller. BR MED J 1:257-262, February 4, 1967.

"Depression and attempted suicide of 91 cases seen in
a casualty department," by J. Birtchnell, et al.
BR J PSYCHIAT 118:289-296, March, 1971.

"Depression and suicide," by H. Ganguly. J IND MED ASS
59:525, December 16, 1972.

"Depression and suicide," by D. J. Lewis. APPL THERAP 9:990-993, December, 1967.

"Depression and suicide," by R. S. Mintz. INT PSYCHIAT CLIN 3:183-195, Winter, 1966.

"Depression and suicide in general medical practice," by W. Offenkranz. AM PRACT 13:427-430, July, 1962.

"Depression and suicide. On some particularly high risk suicidal patients," by G. J. Sarwer-Foner. DIS NERV SYST 30:SUPP: 104-110, February, 1969.

"Depression -- the commonest disease (2) suicide," by P. G. Edgell. CAN MED ASS J 106:175-179, January 22, 1972.

"A study on the relationship between suicidal thoughts and other symptoms in depressive illness," by S. Deb, et al. IND MED ASS 59:507-508, December 16, 1972.

"Suicidal and depressive feelings among college students," by D. C. Murray. PSYCHOL REP 33:175-181, August, 1973.

"Suicide, a hazard in depression," by F. J. Ayd, Jr. J NEUROPSYCHIAT 2(SUPP): 52-54, February, 1961.

"Suicide among patients with diagnosis of anxiety re- action or depressive reaction in general medical and surgical hospitals," by N. Farberow, et al. J ABNORM PSYCHOL 71:287-299, August, 1966.

"Suicide attempts following acute depression," by E. S. Paykel, et al. J NERV MENT DIS 153:234-243, October, 1971.

"Treatment of depression," by M. Hardial. NT 69:741- 743, June 7, 1973.

"Treatment of depression in relation to suicidal attempts," by A. Nomura. DIS NERV SYST 21:701- 703, December, 1960.

MOTIVATION: DEPRESSION IN CHILDREN

MOTIVATION: DEPRESSION IN CHILDREN
  "And children despair," EMERG MED 4:26-27, January,
    1972.

  "Suicide and depression in children," by J. L. Des-
    pert. NERV CHILD 9 NO. 4: 378-389, 1952.

  "Suicide and depression in children," by D. C. Ren-
    shaw. J SCH HEALTH 44:487-489, November, 1974.

MOTIVATION: ECONOMICS: INCOME
  "Effect of income on the suicide rate: a paradox
    resolved," by J. L. Simon. AM J SOCIOL 74:302-3,
    November, 1968.

  "Income, unemployment, and suicide: an occupational
    study," by W. A. Rushing. SOCIOL Q 9:193-503,
    Autumn, 1968.

MOTIVATION: ECONOMICS: INDUSTRIAL PROBLEMS
  "Suicide during productive years: an industrial
    problem," by M. R. Gasque, et al. ARCHIVES
    ENVIRONMENTAL HEALTH 2:457-61, April, 1961.

MOTIVATION: ECONOMICS: RATES OF SUICIDE
  "Economic cycle and the social suicide rate," by
    A. Pierce. AM SOCIOL R 32:457-62, June, 1967.

  "Suicide during productive years: an industrial
    problem," by M. R. Gasque, et al. ARCHIVES
    ENVIRONMENTAL HELATH 2:457-61, April, 1961.

  "Suicide, homocide, and economic development," by
    R. Quinney. SOC FORCES 43:401-6, March, 1965.

MOTIVATION: ECONOMICS: THEORY OF SUICIDE
  "Economic theory of suicide,"by D. S. Hamermesh,et al.
    J POL ECON 82:83-98, January, 1974.

  "National rates of economic growth, anxiety and
    suicide," by R. Lynn. NATURE (London) 222:494,
    May 3, 1969.

MOTIVATION: ECONOMICS: UNEMPLOYMENT
"Suicide and unemployment. A re-examination,"
  by D. Lester. ARCH ENRIRON HELATH (Chicago)
  20:277-8, February, 1970.

"Suicide and unemployment in Pennsylvania," by
  R. Walbran, et al. ARCHIVES ENVIRON HEALTH 10:11-
  15, January, 1965.

"Unemployment and suicide," BRIT MED J 2:965,
  October 22, 1966.

MOTIVATION: FAMILY RELATIONSHIPS
"Attempted suicides from intact and broken parental
  homes," by S. Greer, et al. BRIT MED J 2:1355-7,
  December 3, 1966.

"Broken homes and attempted and completed suicide,"
  by T. L. Dorpat, et al. ARCH GEN PSYCHIAT
  (Chicago) 12:213-6, February, 1965.

"Comment on Jack Gibbs 'Marital status and suicide',"
  by B. E. Segal. AMER J SOCIOL 75:405-11, November, 1969.

"Familial factors in suicide," by R. A. Blath,
  et al. DIS NERV SYST 34:90-3, February, 1973.

"The influence of parental death anniversaries
  upon suicide dates," by J. Bunch, et al. BRIT J
  PSYCHIATRY 118:621-6, June, 1971.

"Marital status and suicide in the United States:
  a special test of the status integration theory,"
  by J. P. Gibbs. AMER J SOCIOL 74:521-33, March,
  1969.

"Parental deprivation and attempted suicide in
  prison populations," by K. M. Koller, et al.
  MED J AUST 1:858-61, April 26, 1969.

"Parental loss and attempted suicide: a further
  report," by S. Greer. BRIT J PSYCHIAT 112:
  465-70, May, 1966.

MOTIVATION: FAMILY RELATIONSHIPS

"Parenthood and suicide: an examination of a
neglect variable," by J. E. Veevers. SOC SCI MED
7:135-44, February, 1973.

"The relationship between parental loss and attempted suicide: a control study," by S. Greer.
BRIT J PSYCHIAT 110:698-705, September, 1964.

"Separation and attempted suicide," by L. D. Levi,
et al. ARCH GEN PSYCHIAT (Chicago) 15:158-64,
August, 1966.

"Sibling position and suicidal behavior," by D.
Lester. J INDIVID PSYCHOL 22:204-7, November,
1966.

"A study on suicides in families of psychotics,"
by S. Tsutumi, et al. BULL OSAKA MED SCH SUPPL
12:399+, 1967.

"Suicidal ideation and parental loss. A preliminary
research report," by K. S. Adam, et al. CAN PSYCHIATR
ASSOC J 18:95-100, April, 1973.

"Suicide and family disorganization," by J. Tuckman,
et al. INT J SOC PSYCHIAT 12:187-91, Summer, 1966.

"Suicide in the widowed," by B. MacMahon, et al.
AM J EPIDEM 81:23-31, January, 1965.

"Suicide of the spouse as a divorce substitute,"
by W. Simon, et al. DIS NERV SYST 31:608-12,
September, 1970.

"Suicide, psychiatrists and therapeutic abortion,"
by A. J. Rosenberg, et al. CALIF MED 102:407-
11, June, 1965.

"Suicide: the role of hostility and death wishes
from the family and significant others," by M.
Rosenbaum, et al. AMER J PSYCHIAT 126:1652-5,
May, 1970.

MOTIVATION: FEMALES
"Completed suicide and females in the labor force,"
by D. Lester. PSYCHOL REP 32:730, June, 1973.

MOTIVATION: FEMALES

"Deviance as therapy: the paradox of the self-
destructive female," by R. W. Maris. J HEALTH
SOC BEHAV 12:113-24, June, 1971.

"Doctors' wives tackle the suicide problem," by
M. Benson. TODAY'S HEALTH 42:60-3, May, 1964.

"The identification of suicidal behavior in females
by the use of the Rorschach," by C. Neuringer,
et al. J GEN PSYCHOL 72:127-33, January, 1965.

"Suicide and women," by E. Hardwick. MADEMOISELLE
76:158-9+, December, 1972.

"Suicide: growing menace to black women," by J.
Slater. EBONY 28:152-4+, September, 1973.

"Women in the labor force and suicide," by J. F.
Newman, et al. SOC PROB 21:220-30, Fall, 1973.

"Women suicide increase due to social pressures,"
SCI N L 85:271, April 25, 1964.

MOTIVATION: FULL MOON
"Association between a full moon and completed
suicide," by D. Lester, et al. PSYCHOL REP
25:598, October, 1969.

"Geomagnetic fluctuations and disturbed behavior,"
by A. D. Pokorny, et al. J NERV MENT DIS 143:
140-51, August, 1966.

MOTIVATION: GENERAL
"Motives for suicide," SCI N L 65:411, June 26,
1954.

"Motivational aspects of suicide in patients during
and after psychiatric treatment," by W. D. Wheat.
SOUTHERN MED J 53:273-8, March, 1960.

MOTIVATION: HOMICIDE
"Cry wolf: a case study of suicide and homicide,"
by S. W. Weiss. DELAWARE MED J 35:293-7, November, 1963.

"Epidemiology of suicide, homicide and accidents,"
by D. N. Pal. INDIAN J MED SCI 21:117-22, February,
1967.

"Homicide and suicide in a metropolitan county.
Long-term trends," by C. S. Hirsch, et al. JAMA
223:900-5, February 19, 1973.

"Homicide, suicide and accidental deaths among nar-
cotic addicts," by M. M. Baden. HUM PATHOL 3:91-
5, March, 1972.

"National homicide and suicide rates as a function
of political stability," by D. Lester. PSYCHOL
REP 33:298, August, 1973.

"Suicide and homicide. An analysis in two countries,"
by H. Hartmann. POST-GRAD MED 40:A20 passim, December, 1966.

"Suicide and homicide by automobile," by J. M.
Macdonald. AMER J PSYCHIAT 121:366-70, October,
1964.

"Suicide and homicide in open and closed societies,"
by D. Lester. PSYCHOL REP 29:430, October, 1971.

"Suicides and homicides among Indians," by M. Ogden,
et al. PUBLIC HEALTH REP 85:75-80, January, 1970.

"Suicide by means of victim-precipitated homicide,"
by M. E. Wolfgang. J CLIN EXP PSYCHOPATH 20:
335-49, October, 1959.

"Suicide, homicide, and color-shading response on
the Rorschach," by D. Lester, et al. PERCEPT MOT
SKILLS 35:562, October, 1972.

"Sunspots, suicide, and homicide," by A. D. Pokorny.
DIS NERV SYST 27:347-8, May, 1966.

"Traffic fatalities, suicide, and homicide," by
A. L. Porterfield. AM SOCIOL R 25:897-901, December, 1960.

MOTIVATION: INHERITED
"Note on the inheritance of suicide," by D. Lester.
PSYCHOL REP 22:320, February, 1968.

MOTIVATION: INSURANCE
"Insurability and suicidal behaviors: issues for
the seventies," by H. L. Resnik, et al. TRANS
ASSOC LIFE INS MED DIR AM 55:132-48, 1972.

MOTIVATION: MEDIA
"Suicide and newspapers: a replicated study," by
S. Blumenthal, et al. AM J PSYCHIATRY 130:468-
71, April, 1973.

"Three suicides laid to TV series of med programs,"
NEW YORK TIMES 26:5, April 9, 1958.

MOTIVATION: MENSTRUATION
"The menstrual cycle and suicide," by J. N. McClure,
Jr., et al. BR J PSYCHIATRY 119:586-7, November,
1971.

"Phase of the menstrual cycle and self-referrals to
a suicide prevention service," by R. D. Wetzel,
et al. BR J PSYCHIATRY 119:523-4, November, 1971.

"Suicide and the menstrual cycle," by A. J.
Mandell, et al. JAMA 200:792-3, May 29, 1967.

"Suicide and the menstrual cycle: a review,"
by R. D. Wetzel, et al. COMPR PSYCHIATRY 13:
369-74, July-August, 1972.

MOTIVATION: MIGRATION
"Migration and suicide," by D. Lester. MED J AUST
1:941-2, April 29, 1972.

"Migration and suicide," by F. A. Whitlock. MED J
AUST 2:840-8, October 23, 1971.

"Suicide and migration," by O. Maller. ISRAEL ANN
PSYCHIAT 4:67-77, Spring, 1966.

MOTIVATION: OCCUPATION
"Jobless suicides," SCI AM 209:68, July, 1963.

MOTIVATION: OCCUPATION

"Occupation and suicide," by T. Tuckman, et al.
  IND MED 33:818-20, November, 1964.

"Occupation, status and suicide: toward a re-
  definition of anomie," by E. H. Powell. AM SOCIOL
  R 23:131-9, April, 1958; "Discussion," AM SOCIOL R
  23:579; 24:86; 250-2, 392-6, October, 1958, February-
  June, 1959.

"Occupational mobility and suicide among white
  males," by W. Breed. AM SOCIOL R 28:179-88, April,
  1963.

"Occupational prestige and social mobility of suicides
  in New Zealand," by A. L. Porterfield, et al. AM
  J SOCIOL 66:147-52, September, 1960.

"Suicide and jobless rates closely related," SCI
  N L 83:296, May 11, 1963.

"Suicide, homicide, and economic development," by
  R. Quinney. SOCIAL FORCES 43:401-6, March, 1965.

"Symposium: psychosocial factors in intensive-
  care nursing. Management of the serious ICU
  nursing problem," by J. Holland, et al. HEART
  LUNG 2:376-81, May-June, 1973.

"Suicide during productive years. An industrial
  problem," by M. R. Gasque, et al. ARCH ENVIRON
  HEALTH (Chicago) 2:457-61, April, 1961.

MOTIVATION: PHYSICAL ILLNESS
  "Chronic dialysis patients: suicide incidence rates,"
  by F. Cutter, et al. AM J PSYCHIATRY 128:495-7,
  October, 1971.

"Chronic disease in former college students. Pre-
  cursors of suicide in early and middle life," by
  R. S. Paffenbarger, Jr., et al. AMER J PUBLIC
  HEALTH 56:1026-36, July, 1966.

"Physical disease, hypochondria, and alcohol addiction
  in suicides committed by mental hospital patients,"
  by A. Stenback, et al. BRIT J PSYCHIAT 111:933-7,
  October, 1965.

MOTIVATION: PHYSICAL ILLNESS

"Suicidal behavior after restoration of sight," by
D. Lester. JAMA 214:916, November 2, 1970.

"Suicidal behavior in chronic dialysis patients,"
by H. S. Abram, et al. AM J PSYCHIATRY 127:1199-
204, March, 1971.

"Suicide after restoration of sight," by D. Lester.
JAMA 219:757, February, 1972.

"Suicide among patients with cardiorespiratory ill-
nesses," by L. Farberow, et al. JAMA 195:422-
8, February 7, 1966.

"Suicide and physical illness," by J. Tuckman, et al.
J GEN PSYCHOL 75:291-5, October, 1966.

"Suicide and primary affective disorders," by S. B.
Guze, et al. BR J PSYCHIATRY 117:437-8, October,
1970.

"Suicide and urinary tract infections," by S. H.
Rosenthal, et al. AMER J PSYCHIAT 122:574-6,
November, 1965.

"Suicide attempts related to congenital facial de-
formities. Two unusual case reports," by J. C.
Berger. PLAST RECONTR SURG 51:323-5, March, 1973.

"Suicide in chronic hemodialysis patients from an
external locus of control framework," by A. M.
Goldstein, et al. AM J PSYCHIATRY 127:1204-7,
March, 1971.

"Suicide. The influence of organic disease," by
I. Stewart. LANCET 2:919-20, October 22, 1960.

MOTIVATION: PREGNANCY
"Abortion and suicidal behaviors: observations on
the concept of 'endangering the mental health of
the mother'," by H. L. Resnik, et al. MENT HYG
55:10-20, January, 1971.

"Maternal deaths involving suicide," OHIO MED J
62:1294-5, December, 1966.

MOTIVATION: PREGNANCY

"Suicide in pregnancy," by C. B. Goodhart. BRIT
MED J 1:318, February 3, 1968.

MOTIVATION: PRISON
"Affective and suicidal symptoms in epileptic
prisoners," by J. Gunn. PSYCHOL MED 5:108-14,
February, 1973.

"America's Devil's Island: inside the Army stockade
at San Francisco's presidio," by D. Duncan.
RAMP MAG 7:8+, January 2, 1969.

"In prison contagion of suicide," by S. Christianson.
NATION 219:243-4, September 21, 1974.

"No one cares: suicides at Rikers Island Peni-
tentiary," NEWSWEEK 75:51-2, March 2, 1970.

"POW's: the aftermath," NEWSWEEK 81:81, June 18,
1973.

"Prison suicides: no cause for concern?," ECONOMIST
231:20+, April 19, 1969.

"Suicide attempts in a Federal prison," by W.
Rieger. ARCH GEN PSYCHIATRY 24:532-5, June, 1971.

MOTIVATION: RACE
"Black suicide," by H. Hendin. ARCH GEN PSYCHIAT
(Chicago) 21:407-22, October, 1969.

"Epidemiological differences between white and non-
white suicide attempters," by A. M. Pederson,
et al. AM J PSYCHIATRY 130:1071-6, October, 1973.

MOTIVATION: RELIGION
"Church and suicide: a common service?," ECONOMIST
205:26+, October 6, 1962.

"Concerning suicide: Anglican committee report,"
TIME 74:74+, November 2, 1959.

"Elementary sin," by J. D. O'Hara. NEW REPUB 166:
29-32, April 22, 1972.

MOTIVATION: RELIGION

"Meaningful death," by J. C. Evans. CHR CENT 82:1598, December 29, 1965.

"Nobility of paganism," AMERICA 97:8, April 6, 1957.

"Religion and attempted suicide," by J. A. Morphew. INT J SOC PSYCHIAT 14:188-192, Summer, 1968.

"Religious beliefs of suicidal patients," by L. Kranitz, et al. PSYCHOL REP 22:936, June, 1968.

"Sacred suicide," by A. Mazrui. ATLAS 11:164-169, March, 1966.

"Sin or a right?" by H. Epstein. NEW YORK TIMES MAG 91+, September 8, 1974.

"Suicide: need for a significant other," by E. T. Culver. CHR CENT 86:100-102, January 15, 1969.

"Thrill seekers mark a decline and fall," CHR CENT 73: 1413-1414, December 5, 1956.

"Ultimately sorrowful," CHR CENT 84:1415, November 1, 1967.

"West religion condemns suicide while Japan considers it morally permissible," NEW YORK TIMES 44:2, April 29, 1972.

MOTIVATION: SACRIFICE
"Sacrificial suicide," by T. Beeson. CHR CENT 91: 836-837, September 18, 1974.

MOTIVATION: SEASONS
"Seasonal variation in suicidal deaths," by D. Lester. BRIT J PSYCHIAT 118:627-628, June, 1971.

"Seasonal variations in suicide rates," by D. Lester. LANCET 1:611-612, March 17, 1963.

"Seasonal variation in suicide rates," by P. S. Spiers. LANCET 2:428-429, August, 1972.

MOTIVATION: SEASONS

"Seasonal variation of suicide and depression," by
W. W. Zung, et al. ARCH GEN PSYCHIAT 30:89-91,
January, 1974.

MOTIVATION: SEXUALITY
"Dual suicide in homosexuals," by M. Swartzburg, et al.
J NERV MENT DIS 155:125-130, August, 1972.

"Sex, marital status and suicide," by W. R. Gove. J
HEALTH SOC BEHAV 13:204-213, June, 1972.

MOTIVATION: STATUS
"Status integration and suicide," by D. Lester. PSYCH-
OL REP 26:492, April, 1970.

"Status integration and suicide: an assessment," by
W. J. Chambliss, et al. AM SOCIOL REV 31:524-532,
August, 1966.

MOTIVATION: SURVIVORS
"The aftermath of suicide," by D. Shepherd, et al. BRIT
MED J 2:600-603, June 15, 1974.

"Psychological resynthesis: a clinical approach to the
survivors of a death by suicide," by H. L. Resnik.
INT PSYCHIAT CLIN 6:213-224, 1969.

MOTIVATION: WEATHER
"Suicide and weather: effect of barometric pressure
and humidity," by A. D. Pokorny. ARCH ENVIRON HEALTH
13:255-256, August, 1966.

"Suicide: seasonal patterns and related variables," by
D. E. Sanborn, 3rd. DIS NERV SYST 31:702-704, October,
1970.

"Suicide, suicide attempts and weather," by A. D. Pokorny, et al. AM J PSYCHIAT 120:377-381, October,
1963.

NOTES
"An analysis of the verbal content of suicide notes,"
by L. A. Gottschalk, et al. BRIT J MED PSYCHOL 33:
195-204, 1960.

NOTES

"A comparison of single and multiple note writers among
suicides," by J. Tuckman, et al. J CLIN PSYCHOL 24:
179-180, April, 1968.

"Credibility of suicide notes," by J. Tuckman, et al.
AM J PSYCHIAT 116:1104-1106, June, 1960.

"Differentiation of simulated and genuine suicide notes,"
By S. A. Arbelt, et al. PSYCHOL REP 33:283-297, August,
1973.

"Effect of foreknowledge of sex and manner of death in
the assessment from suicide notes of intent to die,"
by R. W. Hood, Jr. J SOC PSYCHOL 84:73-80, June,
1971.

"An investigation of handwriting of suicidal persons
through suicide notes," by C. J. Frederick. J ABNORM
PSYCHOL 73:263-267, June, 1968.

"Need for affiliation in suicide notes," by D. Lester.
PERCEPT MOT SKILLS 33:550, October, 1971.

"Phenomenological study of suicide notes," by J. Jacobs.
SOC PROB 15:60-72, Summer, 1967.

"Study of psychological content in the communications
of suicidal individuals," by A. R. Darbonne. J CONSULT
CLIN PSYCHOL 33:590-596, October, 1969.

"Suicide and age: a suicide note analysis," by A. R.
Darbonne. J CONSULT CLIN PSYCHOL 33:46-50, February,
1969.

"Suicide notes and risk of future suicide," by R. W.
Beck, et al. JAMA 228:495-496, April 22, 1974.

"Suicide notes are dull," SCI DIG 76:77, November, 1974.

NURSING
"Attempted suicide and the general nurse," by C. M.
Wallace. NM 128:19, March 14, 1969.

"Attempted suicide and the nursing and medical pro-
fessions," by R. A. Hunt AUST NURS J 2:22, November,
1973.

NURSING

"Bases for nursing assistance to patients being treated
of stenosis of the esophagus caused by intentional
ingestion of caustic soda," by D. R. Cardoso. REV
ESC ENFERM USP 7:196-201, September, 1973.

"Caring for the drug-poisoned patient," by Horgan. RN
25:62+, June, 1962.

"The cry for help!" N FORUM 3:91.#1, 1964.

"Drug overdose," by L. Brown, et al. U NA NURS J 69:
8-17, July, 1971.

"From communications to coordination," by Bergman.
CAN NURS 63:34+, April, 1967.

"Intensive care: a crisis situation," by Woodforde.
AUST NURS J 65:50+, March, 1967.

"Management of the serious suicide attempt: a special
ICU nursing problem," by J. Holland, et al. HEART
LUNG 2:376-381, May-June, 1973.

"Nurse, I need help: the school nurse's role in suicide
prevention," by K. B. Bloomquist. J PSYCHIAT NURS
12:22-26, January-February, 1974.

"The nurse in suicide prevention," by Wallace. NO 15:
55+, March, 1967.

"The nurse's role in preventing suicide," by Rykken.
NO 6:377-378, July, 1958.

"The nurse's role in the prevention of suicide," by
N. L. Farberow, et al. N FORUM 3:93-103, 1964.

"Nursing approaches to the suicidal patient," by Parley.
RN 31:54+, May, 1968.

"Nursing care of the suicidal patient," by Bray, et al.
NM 126:44+, June 14, 1968.

"Nursing care of the suicidal patient," by M. D. Leslie.
CAN NURS 62:39-41, February, 1966.

OTHER COUNTRIES: AFGHANISTAN
"Suicide in Afghanistan," by A. H. Gobar. BRIT J
PSYCHIAT 116:493-496, May, 1970.

OTHER COUNTRIES: AUSTRIA
"Suicides in Los Angeles and Vienna. An intercultural
study of two cities," by N. L. Farberow, et al.
PUBLIC HEALTH REP 84:389-403, May, 1969.

OTHER COUNTRIES: AUSTRALIA
"Alcohol and suicide in Western Australia," by I. P.
James. AUST NZ J PSYCHIAT 5:228, September, 1971.

"Age-sex variations in suicide in Western Australia,"
by P. W. Burvill. MED J AUST 2:1113-1116, December
12, 1970.

"The epidemiology of suicidal behavior in Australia,"
by B. S. Hetzel. AUST NZ J PSYCHIAT 5:156-166,
September, 1971.

"Historical note on completed suicides in Australia:
introduction," by A. Stoller, et al. MED J AUST 1:
334-335, February 12, 1972.

"Methods of suicide in Western Australia," by P. W.
Burvill. MED J AUST 2:411-414, August 29, 1970.

"Rise and fall of suicide rates in Australia: relation
to sedative availability," by R. G. Oliver, et al.
MED J AUST 2:919-923, October 21, 1972.

"Suicide and attempted suicide in Brisbane," by J. E.
Edwards, et al. MED J AUST 1:932-938, June 1, 1968.

"Suicide in Australia," by E. G. Saint. MED J AUST
1:911-920, June 19, 1965.

"Suicide in the Auckland area," by J. S. Lindsay. NZ
MED J 77:149-157, March, 1973.

"Suicide in Western Australia, 1967. An analysis of
coroners' records," by P. W. Burvil. AUST NZ J PSYCH-
IAT 5:37-44, March, 1971.

OTHER COUNTRIES: BAHAMAS

OTHER COUNTRIES: BAHAMAS
   "Suicide in the Bahamas," by D. J. Spencer.   INT J SOC
      PSYCHIAT 18:110-113, Summer, 1972.

OTHER COUNTRIES: BALI
   "Ballet of death in Bali," by J. Carlova.   CORONET 43:
      108-111, February, 1958.

OTHER COUNTRIES: BRITAIN
   "Attempted suicide in Newcastle upon Tyne," by F. A.
      Whitlock, et al. BRIT J PSYCHIAT 113:423-434, April,
      1967.

   "Bodies in the West London Thames," by G. Thurston.
      MEDICOLEGAL J 28:193-199, 1960.

   "Changes in the pattern of admissions for attempted
      suicide in Newcastle upon Tyne during the 1960's,"
      by J. S. Smith, et al. BR MED 4:412-415, November
      13, 1971.

   "Deliberate self-injury (attempted suicide) in patients
      admitted to hospital in Mid-Sussex," by S. Jacobson,
      et al. BRIT J PSYCHIAT 121:379-386, October, 1972.

   "Deliberate self-poisoning in the Oxford area," by J.
      G. Evans. BRIT J PREV SOC MED 21:97-107, July, 1967.

   "A review of 216 cases of attempted suicide in a Brit-
      ish hospital," by I. S. Menon. J IND MED ASS 47: 22-
      26, July 1, 1966.

   "Student suicides cause concern in England," SCI N L
      75:185, March 21, 1959.

   "Suicide and mortality amongst heroin addicts in Brit-
      ain," by J. Pierce. BRIT J ADDICT 52:391-398, Decem-
      ber, 1967.

   "Suicide -- English style," by G. Day. PERS BIOL MED
      14:290-300, Winter, 1971.

   "Suicide in Brighton," by S. Jacobson, et al. BRIT J
      PSYCHIAT 121:369-377, October, 1972.

OTHER COUNTRIES: BRITAIN

"Suicide in Bristol," by C. P. Seager, et al. BRIT J
PSYCHIAT 111:919-932, October, 1965.

"Suicide in England and Wales 1959-1963. The country
boroughs," by F. A. Whitlock. PSYCHOL MED 3:35-65,
August, 1973.

"Suicide in South London. An analysis of the admissions for attempted suicide in one medical unit of a
general hospital," by D. J. Taylor, et al. PRACT
192-251-256, February, 1964.

"Suicide rate in Britain," by D. Lester. LANCET 1:899,
April 22, 1972.

OTHER COUNTRIES: CANADA
"Suicide in Canada -- trends and preventive aspects,"
by F. A. Allodi, et al CAN MENTAL HEALTH 21:15-16,
September-October, 1973.

OTHER COUNTRIES: CEYLON
"In Ceylon," by N. D. Gunasekara. J CEYLON BRIT MED
ASS 46:138-148, December, 1951.

"Status integration and suicide in Ceylon," by J. P.
Gibbs, et al. AM J SOC 64:585-591, May, 1959.

"Suicide, homicide, and social structure in Ceylon,"
by J. H. Straus, et al. AM J SOC 58:461-469, March,
1953.

OTHER COUNTRIES: CHILE
"Suicide in Santiago, Chile," by C. Chuaqui, et al.
PUBLIC HEALTH REP 81:1109-1117, December, 1966.

OTHER COUNTRIES: DENMARK
"Durkheim, Denmark and suicide: a sociological inter-
pretation of statistical data (findings of Emile
Durkheim reviewed)," by H. P. Weiss. ACTA SOCIOLOG-
ICA 7:261-278, 1964.

"Melancholy Danes," NEWSWEEK 58:75, August 7, 1961.

OTHER COUNTRIES: DENMARK

"Suicide frequency before and after introduction of
community psychiatry in a Danish island," by J. Niel-
sen, et al. BRIT J PSYCHIAT 123:35-39, July, 1973.

"Suicide in Denmark," by H. Hendin. COLUMBIA U FORUM
4:26-32, Summer, 1961.

"Suicide in Denmark," by H. Hendin. PSYCHIAT Q 34:443-
460, July, 1960.

"Suicide in Denmark," by H. Hendin. PSYCHIAT Q 34:443-
460, July, 1960.

"Suicides in Denmark," by K. Rudfeld. ACTA SOCIOLOGICA
6:203-214, 1962.

OTHER COUNTRIES: FIJI
"Suicide in Macuata province, Fiji. A review of 73
cases," by G. H. Ree. PRACT 207:669-671, November,
1971.

OTHER COUNTRIES: FINLAND
"On suicides committed under the influence of alcohol
in Finland in 1967," by M. Virkkunen, et al. BRIT J
ADDICT 65:317-313, December, 1970.

OTHER COUNTRIES: FRANCE
"The suicide problem in French sociology," by A. Giddens. BRIT J SOC 16:3-18, March, 1965.

OTHER COUNTRIES: GENERAL
"Analysis of rates in selected countries, specific for
age and sex," by P. W. Burvill. INT J SOC PSYCHIAT
18:137-139, Summer, 1972.

"Clues to suicide," by E. S. Shneidman, et al. PUBLIC
HEALTH REP 71:109-114, February, 1956.

"Community growth, depressive disorders, and suicide,"
by H. Wechsler. AM J SOC 67:9-16, July, 1961.

"Cross-cultural studies," by H. Hendin. PSYCHIAT DIG
26:25-34, January, 1965.

OTHER COUNTRIES: GENERAL

"Growing cities and human happiness," WORLD HEALTH
17:29+, January, 1964.

"A high incidence of suicide in a preliterate-prim-
itive society," by J. O. Hoskin, et al. PSYCHIAT
32:200-210, May, 1969.

"Mortality from suicide in selected countries since
beginning of century," EPIDEMIOL & VITAL STATIS REP
9:250-279, 1956.

"Number of suicides in selected countries since beginning of century," EPIDEMIOL & VITAL STATIS REP 9:
244-249, 1956.

"Suicide -- a world problem," LANCET 2:1411, December
25, 1971.

"Suicide: an instance of high rural rates," by W. W.
Schroeder, et al. RURAL SOCIOL 18:45-52, March, 1953.

"Suicide and mutilation behaviors in non-literate societies," by D. Lester. PSYCHOL REP 28:801-802,
June, 1971.

"Suicide in a 'welfare state'," by G. Paerregaard.   INT
ANESTH CLIN 4:373-377, Summer, 1966.

"Suicide in Europe," by T. B. Hauschild.   MED BULL US
ARMY EUROPE   21:250-254, August, 1964.

"Suicide -- international comparisons,"   STATIS BULL
METROP LIFE INS CO 53:2-5, August, 1972.

OTHER COUNTRIES: GERMANY
"Berlin suicide rate," NEW YORK TIMES 10:7, December
22, 1952.

"Berlin syndrome," TIME 95:92, March 30, 1970.

OTHER COUNTRIES: INDIA
"Disorganization: its role in Indian suicide rates,"
by J. Westermeyer. AM J PSYCHIAT 128:123-124, July,
1971.

OTHER COUNTRIES: INDIA

"An epidemetric study of suicides in Nagpur City for
the quinquennium 1953 to 1957," by D. K. Ramadwar,
et al. IND J PUBLIC HEALTH 13:144-149, July, 1969.

"A study of suicide in Delhi state," by K. Singh, et
al. J IND MED ASS 57:412-419, December 1, 1971.

"A study of suicide in Maudurai," by M. N. Ganapathi,
et al. J IND MED ASS 46:18-23, January 1, 1966.

"The suicide problem in India," by R. E. Pandey.   INT
J SOC PSYCHIAT 14:193-200, Summer, 1968.

OTHER COUNTRIES: IRELAND
"Attempted suicide before and after the communal violence in Belfast, August, 1969. A preliminary study,"
by P. P. O'Malley. J IR MED ASS 65:109-113, March 4,
1972.

"Attempted suicide in Dublin," by P. D. McCarthy, et al.
J IRISH MED ASS 57:8-13, July, 1965.

"Suicide in Dublin," by P. D. McCarthy, et al. BRIT MED
J 5500:1393-1396, June 4, 1966.

OTHER COUNTRIES: ISRAEL
"Aspects of suicide in Israel," by I. Drapkin. ISRAEL
ANN PSYCHIAT 3:35-50, April, 1965.

"Comparative epidemiologic aspects of suicide in Israel,"
by B. Modan, et al. AM J EPIDEM 91:393-399, April,
1970.

OTHER COUNTRIES: ITALY
"Suicides in Italy and abroad: trend over the past ten
years," ITAL AFFAIRS 11:3845-3848, March-April, 1962.

OTHER COUNTRIES: JAPAN
"Cultural factors in suicide of Japanese youth with
focus on personality," by M. Iga. SOCIOL & SOC RES
46:75-90, October, 1961.

"Death under the cherry blossom," ECONOMIST 187:324+,
April 26, 1958.

OTHER COUNTRIES: JAPAN

"Examination hell: Japan's student suicides," TIMES ED
SUPP 2475:533, October 26, 1962.

"Harakiri and suicide by sharp instruments in Japan,"
by T. Watanabe, et al. FORENS SCI 2:191-199, May,
1973.

"Japanese suicides during World War II," NEW YORK TIMES
7:6, December 29, 1953.

"Letter from Japan," by D. Richie. NATION 187:98-100,
August 30, 1958.

"The psychopathology of suicide in Japan," by L. Beall.
INT J SOC PSYCHIAT 14:213-225, Summer, 1968.

"Public welfare in Japan," TIME 58:34, July 2, 1951.

"Relation of suicide attempt and social structure in
Kamakura, Japan," by M. Iga. INT J SOC PSYCHIAT
12:221-232, Summer, 1966.

"Suicide attempts of Japanese youth and Durkheim's concept of anomie: an interpretation," by M. Iga, et al.
HUM ORGAN 26:59-68, Spring/Summer, 1967.

"Suicide in Japan," AMERICA 98:388, January 4, 1958.

"Young love in Japan," TIME 65:32, January 17, 1955.

"Young love versus Japan's old code," by R. Trumbull.
NY TIMES MAG 26+, March 9, 1958.

OTHER COUNTRIES: MALAYA
"Suicide attempters admitted to the University of Malaya
Medical Center Psychiatric Unit," by R. C. Simons,
et al. INT J SOC PSYCHIAT 18:97-103, Summer, 1972.

OTHER COUNTRIES: NEW GUINEA
"Suicide in Papua and New Guinea," by N. Parker, et al.
MED J AUST 2:1125-1128, December 10, 1966.

OTHER COUNTRIES: NEW ZEALAND
"Occupational prestige and social mobility of suicides
in New Zealand," by A. L. Porterfield, et al. AM J
SOCIOL 66:147-152, September, 1960.

OTHER COUNTRIES: NIGERIA
"Suicide in Western Nigeria," by T. Asuni. BRIT
MED J 5312:1091-7, October 27, 1962.

"Suicide in Western Nigeria," by T. Asuni. INT J
PSYCHIAT 1:52-63, January, 1965.

"Suicidal gestures in occupation personnel on
Okinawa," by L. G. Laufer, et al. U S ARMED
FORCES M J 3:1825-30, December, 1952.

"Suicide in Okinawa: preliminary explorations,"
by T. W. Maretzki. INT J SOC PSYCHIAT 11:256-
63, Autumn, 1965.

OTHER COUNTRIES: PANAMA
"Suicide, sacrifice and mutilations in burials at
Venado Beach, Panama," by S. K. Lothrop. AM ANTIQ
19:226-34, January, 1954.

OTHER COUNTRIES: PAPUA
"Suicide in Papua and New Guinea," by N. Parker,
et al. MED J AUST 2:1125-8, December 10, 1966.

OTHER COUNTRIES: PUERTO RICO
"Suicide attempts of Puerto Rican immigrants," by
by E. C. Trautman. PSYCHIAT QUART 35:544-54,
July, 1961.

OTHER COUNTRIES: SCOTLAND
"Are the Scottish and English suicide rates really
different?," by B. M. Barraclough. BR J PSYCHIATRY
120:267-73, March, 1972.

"Spectrum of suicidal behaviors in Edinburgh," by
I. M. Ovenstone. BR J PREV SOC MED 27:27-35,
February, 1973.

"Suicidal behavior in Edinburgh and Seattle," by
H. S. Ripley. AM J PSYCHIATRY 130:995-1001,
September, 1973.

"Suicide in Scotland in comparison with England
and Wales," by N. Kreitman. BR J PSYCHIATRY 121:
83-7, July, 1972.

OTHER COUNTRIES: SOVIET UNION

OTHER COUNTRIES: SOVIET UNTION
   "Suicides in the Soviet Union: a roster of some who
   sought this escape from communism," by B. Souvarine.
   NEW LEADER   8, September 3, 1956.

OTHER COUNTRIES: SWEDEN
   "I shall jump at one: chimney sweep in Hallstahammar,
   Sweden," LIFE 31:57-8, December 10, 1951.

   "Some cultural determinants of suicide in Sweden,"
   by K. E. Rudstam. J SOC PSYCHOL 80:225-7, April,
   1970.

   "Stockholm and Los Angeles: a cross-cultural study
   of the communication of suicidal intent," by K. E.
   Rudestam. J CONSULT CLIN PSYCHOL 36:82-90, February,
   1971.

   "Suicide in Sweden," by H. Hendin. PSYCHIAT QUART
   36:1-28, January, 1962.

   "Suicide rate in Sweden," NEW YORK TIMES 14:1, March
   27, 1960.

   "Welfare and suicide rate in Sweden," NEW YORK TIMES
   28:5, December 29, 1965.

OTHER COUNTRIES: TASMANIA
   "Epidemiology of drug overdosage in Southern
   Tasmania," by J. W. Freeman, et al. MED J AUST
   2:1168-72, December 19, 1970.

   "In Tasmania," by C. Duncan. MED J AUST   2:166-
   68, July 31, 1954.

OTHER COUNTRIES: VIENNA
   "Morphinist: incident at Hospital of the City of
   Vienna," by R. Berczeller. NEW YORKER 42:141-2+,
   April 16, 1966.

   "Refugee camp attempts," NEW YORK TIMES 30:4,
   April 7, 1957. "Interior Minister denies report,"
   NEW YORK TIMES 5:6, April 9, 1957.

OTHER COUNTRIES: VIETNAM

OTHER COUNTRIES: VIETNAM
  "Suicide in many forms: South Viet Nam," TIME 82:32+,
    July 19, 1963.

OTHER COUNTRIES: WALES
  "Suicide in England and Wales 1959-1963. The county
    boroughs," by F. A. Whitlock. PSYCHOL MED 3:350-365,
    August, 1973.

OVERDOSE
  SEE DRUGS: OVERDOSE

PARASUICIDE: ADOLESCENTS
  "Adolescent suicide attempts. A follow-up study of
    hospitalized patients," by J. T. Barter, et al. ARCH
    GEN PSYCHIAT 40:87-96, January, 1970.

  "Adolescents who attempt suicide: preliminary findings,"
    by J. D. Teicher, et al. AM J PSYCHIAT 122:1248-1257,
    May, 1966.

  "Attempted suicide and self-mutilation in adolescence:
    some observations from a psychoanalytic research
    project," by M. Friedman, et al. INT J PSYCHOANAL
    53:179-183, 1972.

  "Attempted suicide in adolescents," by H. Jacobziner.
    JAMA 191:7-11, January 4, 1965.

  "Attempted suicide in adolescents," by L. A. Senseman.
    R I MED J 51:109-112, February, 1968.

  "Attempted suicide in adolescents," by J. Tuckman, et al.
    AM J PSYCHIAT 119:228-232, September, 1962.

  "Attempted suicide in adolescents by poisoning: statis-
    tical report," by H. Jacobziner. AM J PSYCHOTHER
    19:247-252, April, 1965.

  "Attempted suicide in an adolescent: the resolution of
    an anxiety state," by A. S. Yusin. ADOLESCENCE 8:17-
    28, Spring, 1973.

"Broken homes and social isolation in attempted suicides of adolescents," by J. Jacobs, et al. INT J
SOC PSYCHIAT 13:139-149, Spring, 1967.

"Children and adolescents who attempt suicide," by J.
D. Teicher. PED CLIN N AM 17:687-696, August, 1970.

"Clinical studies of attempted suicide in childhood,"
by R. S. Lourie. CLIN PROC CHILD HOSP (WASH) 22:
163-173, June, 1966.

"I want out: teens who threaten suicide," by H. Pollack.
TODAY'S HEALTH 49:32-34+, January, 1971.

"Latency-age children who threaten or attempt to kill
themselves," by W. C. Ackerly. J AM ACAD CHILD PSYCH-
IAT 6:242-261, April, 1967.

"Management of adolescent suicide attempts," by D. W.
Cline. MINN MED 56:111:113, February, 1973.

"Some typical patterns in the behavior and background
of adolescent girls who attempt suicide," by A.
Schrut. AM J PSYCHIAT 125:69-74, July, 1968.

"Study of social and psycholgical characteristics of adolescent suicide attempters in urban disadvantaged area,"
by B. F. Corder, et al. ADOLESCENCE 9:1-6, Spring, 1974.

"Suicidal attempts in adolescent girls. A preliminary
study," by J. Bigras, et al. CAN PSYCHIAT ASS J 11:
SUPP: 275-282, 1966.

"Suicidal attempts in children," by R. H. Lawler, et
al. CAN MED ASS J 89:751-754, October 12, 1963.

"Suicide and attempted suicide in children and adolescents," by R. S. Lourie. TEXAS MED 63:58-63, November, 1967.

"Suicide and attempted suicide in children and adolescents," by J. H. Yacoubian, et al. CLIN PROC CHILD
HOSP DC 25:325-344, December, 1969.

PARASUICIDE: ADOLESCENTS

"Suicide and suicidal attempts in children and adolescents," LANCET 2:847-848, October 17, 1964.

"Suicide and suicidal attempts in children and adolescents," by J. M. Toolan. AM J PSYCHIAT 118:719-724,
February, 1962.

"Suicide and suicide attempts in a population pregnant
as teenagers," by I. W. Gabrielson, et al. AM J PUBLIC
HEALTH 60:2289-2301, December, 1970.

"Suicide threats and attempts in young: psychologic
management," by D. Powers. AM PRACT & DIGEST TREAT 7:
1140-1143, July, 1956.

"Thirteen adolescent male suicide attempts. Dynamic
considerations," by N. L. Margolin, et al. J AM ACAD
CHILD PSYCHIAT 7:296-315, April, 1968.

PARASUICIDE: CHILDREN
"Child suicide attempts," SCI NL 79:310, May 20, 1961.

"Children and adolescents who attempt suicide," by J.
D. Teicher. PED CLIN N AM 17:687-696, August, 1970.

"Clinical studies of attempted suicide in childhood,"
by R. S. Lourie. CLIN PROC CHILD HOSP (WASH) 22:
163-173, June, 1966.

"Suicidal attempts in children," by R. H. Lawler, et
al. CAN MED ASS J 89:751-754, October 12, 1963.

"Suicide and attempted suicide in children and adolescents," by R. S. Lourie. TEXAS MED 63:58-63, November, 1967.

"Suicide and attempted suicide in children and adolescents," by J. H. Yacoubian, et al. CLIN PROC CHILD
HOSP DC 25:325-344, December, 1969.

"Suicide attempt by a ten-year-old after quadruple
amputations," by H. L. Resnik. JAMA 212:1211-1212,
May 18, 1970.

PARASUICIDE: CRISIS INTERVENTION
"The nursing consultant in a suicide prevention center,"
by K. K. Bell. NURS CLIN N AM 5:687-697, December,
1970.

"The role of the nurse in crisis intervention and
suicide prevention," by C. J. Frederick. J PSYCHIATR
NURS 11:27-31, January-February, 1973.

"The role of the nurse in suicide prevention," by P.
K. Clemons. J PSYCHIATR NURS 9:27-30, January-February, 1971.

"The Samaritans: a nurse's impressions," by Lavinia.
NM 134:26-27, March 31, 1972.

"The suicidal patient in the community: a challenge for
the nurses," by Kloes. ANA CLIN SESSIONS 36+, 1968.

"With suicidal patients: caring for is caring about,"
by T. Umscheid. AM J NURS 67:1230-1232, June, 1967.

PARASUICIDE: GENERAL
"Alcoholism, alcohol intoxication and suicide attempts,"
by D. G. Mayfield, et al. ARCH GEN PSYCHIAT 27:349-
353, September, 1972.

"Assessing attempted suicide," by W. J. Cassidy. HENRY
FORD HOSP MED J 18:205-210, Fall, 1970.

"Attempt: excerpt from The Savage God," by A. Alvarez.
ATLAN 227:84-86+, April, 1971.

"Attempted suicide," by I. R. C. Batchelor. BRIT MED J
1:595-597, March 5, 1955.

"Attempted suicide," by N. J. Browne. MED J AUST 2:1309,
December 18, 1971.

"Attempted suicide," by J. P. Crawford, et al. LANCET
1:499, March 6, 1971.

"Attempted suicide," by N. Kessel. MED WORLD (London)
97:313-322, October, 1962.

PARASUICIDE: GENERAL

PARASUICIDE: GENERAL
"Attempted suicide," by P. M. Last. MED J AUST 1:708-710, April 8, 1967.

"Attempted suicide," by H. Merskey. BRIT J PSYCHIAT 115:1227, October, 1969.

"Attempted suicide," by D. M. Ralph. NT 63:688-690, May 26, 1967.

"Attempted suicide," by C. A. Short. NT 66:1067-1068, August 20, 1970.

"Attempted suicide," by E. Stengel. BRIT J PSYCHIAT 116: 237-238, February, 1970.

"Attempted suicide. A comparative study," by P. K. Bridges, et al. COMPR PSYCHIAT 7:240-247, August, 1966.

"Attempted suicide: a description of the pre and post suicidal states," by J. M. Sendbuehler. CAN PSYCH-IATR ASS J 18:113-116, April, 1973.

"Attempted suicide: a four month study," by N. B. Goss-Moffitt. J KEN MED ASS 61:585-588, July, 1963.

"Attempted suicide: a Sleeping Beauty phenomenon," by L. B. Brown. NEW ZEAL NURS J 63:9-12, January, 1970.

"Attempted suicide -- a study of 100 patients referred to a general hospital," by I. P. James, et al. MED J AUST 50 (1):375-380, March 16, 1963.

"Attempted suicide and body image," by D. Lester. J PSYCHOL 66:287-290, July, 1967.

"Attempted suicide and family disorganization," by J. Tuckman, et al. J GENET PSYCHOL 105:187-193, December, 1964.

"Attempted suicide and social class," by J. Sendbuehler, et al. CAN PSYCHIATR ASS J 17:SUPP 2:SS185, 1972.

"Attempted suicide and suicidal gestures," by W. J. Stanley. BRIT J PREV SOC MED 23:190-195, August, 1969.

"Attempted suicide and the menstrual cycle," by C. M. Tonks, et al. J PSYCHOSOM RES 11:319-323, March, 1968.

"Attempted suicide as a hostile act," by D. Lester. J PSYCHOL 68:243-248, March, 1968.

"Attempted suicide as language: an empirical study," by N. Kreitman, et al. BRIT J PSYCHIAT 116:465-473, May, 1970.

"Attempted suicide by adults," by J. Tuckman, et al. PUBLIC HEALTH REP 77:605-614, July, 1962.

"Attempted suicide during the course of labor," by G. W. Woddis, et al. MEDICO-LEGAL J 28:209-211, 1960.

"Attempted suicide: experience in a general hospital emergency service," by B. R. Shochet. MD MED J 13: 107-112, March, 1964.

"Attempted suicide: facts and theories," by J. M. Send-buehler. DIS NERV SYST 30:SUPP:111-114, February, 1969.

"Attempted suicide in a largely rural area during an eight year period," by H. Hershon. BRIT J PSYCHIAT 114:279-284, March, 1968.

"Attempted suicide in Glasgow," by A. B. Sclare, et al. BRIT J PSYCHIAT 109:609-615, September, 1963.

"Attempted suicide. Its management in the general hospital," by E. Stengel. LANCET 1:233-135, February 2, 1963.

"Attempted suicide: nomenclature," by A. Dodds. BR J PSYCHIAT 117:121, July, 1970.

"Attempted suicide. Some statistical and psychiatric parameters," by J. Sendbuehler, et al. DIS NERV SYST 31:SUPP:59-68, November, 1970.

"Attempted suicides in psychotic patients: dynamic con-cept," by J. D. Waxberg PSYCHIAT Q 30:464-470, July, 1956.

"The changing pattern of attempted suicide in Edinburgh, 1962-1967," by R. C. Aitken, et al. BRIT J PREV SOC MED 23:111-115, May, 1969.

"The chronic wrist-slasher," by H. Graff. HOSP TOP 45: 61-65, November, 1967.

"A comparison of suicidal thinkers and attempters: interim findings," by J. A. Humphrey, et al. DIS NERV SYST 32:825-830, December, 1971.

"Dealing with attempted suicide," by D. H. Ropschitz. BRIT MED J 2:117-118, April 13, 1968.

"Defense styles in suicide attempters," by J. A. Scholz. J CONSULT CLIN PSYCHOL 41:70-73, August, 1973.

"Drug abusers, suicide attempters, and the MMPI," by D. E. Sanborn, 3rd., et al. DIS NERV SYST 32:183-187, March, 1971.

"Depression with attempted suicide treated at general hospital," by A. M. Mann, et al. CAN MED ASS J 68: 381-383, April, 1953.

"Distress behavior: a study of selected Samaritan clients and parasuicides (attempted suicide patients)," by N. Kreitman, et al- BRIT J PSYCHIAT 123:1-8, July, 1973.

"Emergency evaluation of suicide attempters," by R. F. Kraus. PA MED 75:60-62, April, 1972.

"An epidemic of attempted suicide," by L. D. Hankoff. COMPR PSYCHIAT 2:294-298, October, 1961.

"An epidemiological survey of parasuicide (attempted suicide) in general practice," by P. Kennedy, et al. BRIT J PSYCHIAT 123:23-34, July, 1973.

"The epidemiology of attempted suicide as seen in the casualty department, Alfred Hospital, Melbourne," by R. G. Oliver, et al. MED J AUST 1:833-839, April 17, 1971.

"An evaluation of suicidal intent in suicide attempts,"
by T. L. Dorpat, et al. COMPR PSYCHIAT 4:117-125,
April, 1963.

"A follow-up study of wrist slashers," by S. H. Nelson,
et al. AM J PSYCHIAT 127:1345-1349, April, 1971.

"Management of attempted suicide," BRIT MED J 5261:
1202-1203, November 4, 1961.

"Medico-social aspects of attempted suicide," by P.
Beighton, et al. BRIT J CLIN PRACT 21:593-597, December, 1967.

"The motivation and emotional state of 91 cases of
attempted suicide," by J. Birtchnell, et al. BRIT
J MED PSYCHOL 44:45-52, March, 1971.

"Multiple standardization of parasuicide (attempted
suicide) rates in Edinburgh," by D. Buglass, et al.
BRIT J PREV SOC MED 24:182-186, August, 1970.

"The natural history of attempted suicide in Bristol,"
by J. Roberts, et al. BRIT J MED PSYCHOL 42:303-312,
December, 1969.

"No exit: the persistently suicidal patient," by J. S.
Maxmen, et al. COMPR PSYCHIAT 14:71-79, January-February, 1973.

"Parasuicide," by N. Kreitman, et al. BRIT J PSYCHIAT
115:746-747, June, 1969.

"The persistent suicidal patient," by C. Watkins, et al.
AM J PSYCHIAT 125:1590-1593, May, 1969.

"Personality and parasuicide: methodological problems,"
by M. R. Eastwood, et al. MED J AUST 1:170-175, January 22, 1972.

"Pregnancy and attempted suicide," by F. A. Whitlock,
et al. COMPR PSYCHIAT 9:1-12, January, 1968.

"Prognosis and follow-up of attempted suicide," by P.
Udsen. INT ANESTH CLIN 4:379-388, Summer, 1966.

PARASUICIDE: GENERAL

"Pseudosuicide as a symbolic act," by G. Greaves.
PSYCHOL REP 31:280, August, 1972.

"A psychodynamic study of an attempted suicide," by
J. Weisfogel. PSYCHIAT Q 43:257-284, 1969.

"Psychotherapeutic aspects of unsuccessful suicide
attempts," by S. A. Alleman. J AM COLL HEALTH ASS 13:
390-398, February, 1965.

"Recent research into suicide and attempted suicide,"
by E. Stengel. AM J PSYCHIAT 118:725-727, February,
1962.

"Relation between attempted suicide and completed suicide," by D. Lester. PSYCHOL REP 27:719-722, December, 1970.

"Relation of depression of attempted suicide and ser-
iousness of intent," by M. A. Silver, et al. ARCH GEN
PSYCHIAT 25:573-576, December, 1971.

"The relationship between attempted suicide and committed suicide," by T. L. Dorpat, et al. COMPR PSYCHIAT
8:74-79, April, 1967.

"The relationship between attempted suicide and depression and parent death," by J. Birtchnell. BRIT J
PSYCHIAT 116:307-313, March, 1970.

"Repeated attempts (especially in psychopathic and epileptic individuals," by I. R. C. Batchelor. BRIT J
MED PSYCHOL 27:158-163, 1954.

"Risk taking and hedonic mood stimulation in suicide
attempters," by G. E. Kochansky. J ABNORM PSYCHOL 81:
80-86, February, 1973.

"Risk taking in the lives of parasuicides (attempted
suicides)," by P. Kennedy, et al. BRIT J PSYCHIAT 119:
281-286, September, 1971.

"Role of education in reporting attempted suicide," by
D. E. Sanborn, 3rd., et al. DIS NERV SYST 32:467-471,
July, 1971.

PARASUICIDE: GENERAL

"A scale for assessing suicide risk of attempted suicides," by J. Tuckman, et al. J CLIN PSYCHOL 24: 17-19, January, 1968.

"The serious suicide attempt: epidemiological and follow-up study of 886 patients," by D. Rosen. AM J PSYCH-IAT 127:764-770, December, 1970.

"The severe suicide attempter and self-concept," by L. Wilson, et al. J CLIN PSYCHOL 27:307-309, July, 1971.

"Sex differences in suicide and attempted suicide," by F. B. Davis. DIS NERV SYST 29:193-194, March, 1968.

"Suicidal attempts," by M. E. Finn. J NERV & MENT DIS 121:172-176, February, 1955.

"Suicide and attempted suicide in Brisbane," by J. E. Edwards, et al. MED J AUST 1:989-995, June 8, 1968.

"Suicide and attempted suicide: study of perceived sex differences," by M. M. Linehan. PERCEPT MOT SKILLS 37:31-34, August, 1973.

"Suicide and suicide attempts among American Indians of the American Northwest," by J. H. Shore. INT J SOC PSYCHIAT 18:91-96, Summer, 1972.

"Suicide attempt," by S. Brekken. PRAIRIE ROSE 41:9-10, July-September, 1972.

"Suicide attempt," by J. M. Piret. INFIRM 43:38-40, October, 1965.

"Suicide attempt," by H. R. Roberts. NM 129:33-34, September 19, 1969.

"Suicide attempts," BRIT MED J 2:483, May 29, 1971.

"Suicide attempts. A longitudinal view," by J. A. Motto. ARCH GEN PSYCHIAT (CHICAGO) 13:516-520, December, 1965.

"Suicide attempts and psychiatric diagnosis," by R. A. Woodruff, Jr., et al. DIS NERV SYST 33:617-621, September, 1972.

PARASUICIDE: GENERAL

"Suicide attempts. NAMI-975," by G. J. Tucker, et al.
US NAVAL AEROSPACE MED INST 1-19, August, 1966.

"Suicide and pseudosuicide: a reanalysis of Maris' data,"
by R. L. Hamblin, et al. J HEALTH SOC BEHAV 13:99-109,
March, 1972.

"Suicide by poisoning. Some controversial aspects of
attempted suicide," by E. Stengel. NT 61:1143-1144,
August 20, 1965.

"Suicide risk among persons attempting suicide," by J.
Tuckman, et al. PUBLIC HEALTH REP 78:585-587, July,
1963.

"Some characteristics of attempted suicide," by D. Dies-
pecker, et al. MED J AUST 2:121-125, July 21, 1973.

"Some unexplored aspects of suicide and attempted suicide," by E. Stengel. COMPR PSYCHIAT 1:71-79, April,
1960.

"Test-retest characteristics of a group of attempted
suicide patients," by A. E. Philip, et al. J CONSULT.
CLIN PSYCHOL 34:144-147, April, 1970.

"Traits, attitudes and symptoms in a group of attempted
suicides," by A. E. Philip. BRIT J PSYCHIAT 116:475-
482, May, 1970.

"Treatment of suicidal attempts," by G. C. Sisler. CAN
MED ASS J 74:112-115, January 15, 1956.

"Videotape confrontation after attempted suicide," by
H. L. Resnik, et al. AM J PSYCHIAT 130:460-463, April,
1973.

PARASUICIDE: LITERATURE
"Attempt: excerpt from The Savage God," by A. Alvarez.
ATLAN 227:84-86+, April, 1971.

PARASUICIDE: MENTAL ILLNESS
SEE ALSO: MENTAL PATIENTS
"Six aspects of mental illness. Suicide and attempted
suicide. Part 2," by Nixon, et al. NM 119:407+, January 29, 1965.

PARASUICIDE: PATIENTS

PARASUICIDE: PATIENTS
"The patient who tried it and failed," by C. J. Hobson.
RN 29:43-44, March, 1966.

PARASUICIDE: REPORTS, STUDIES, CONFERENCES
"Incompleat suicide: concerning symposium on suicide
held in Washington, D.C., " by M. Huxley. NATION
201:414-417, November 29, 1965.

"Preliminary report of the Rosenzweig study in attempted
suicides," by D. L. Winfield, et al. J CLIN PSYCHOL
9:379-381, October, 1953.

PARASUICIDE: RISKS
"Identifying suicide risk groups among attempted suicides," by Tuckman, et al. PUBLIC HEALTH REP (WASH)
78:763+, September, 1963.

"Suicide risk among persons attempting suicide," by
Tuckman, et al. PUBLIC HEALTH REP (WASH) 78:585+,
July, 1963.

PARASUICIDE: STATISTICS
"Completed and attempted suicides: a comparative analysis," by C. F. Schmid, et al. AM SOCIOL R 20:273-
288, June, 1955.

PARASUICIDE: THREATS
"Threats and meaning," NEWSWEEK 45:74, January 10, 1955.

PHYSICIANS: GENERAL
"Burden of responsibility in suicide and homicide (role
of the physician in prevention and in identification
and treatment of suicidal and homicidal risks)," by
P. Solomon. AM MED ASS J 199:321-324, January 30,
1967.

"Clinical prediction of physician suicide based on
medical student data," by L. C. Epstein, et al. J NERV
MENT DIS 156:19-29, January, 1973.

"Doctors can help prevent suicides by poisoning," SCI
N L 73:338, May 31, 1958.

"Doctors killing themselves," by A. J. Snider. SCI DIG
76:49, October, 1974.

"The doctor/patient relationship in manipulative suicide. A common psychosomatic disease," by P. E.
Sifneos. PSYCHOTHER PSYCHOSOM 18:40-46, 1970.

"The family doctor and the suicidal crisis," by J. M.
Lewis. TEX MED 64:52-56, January, 1968.

"The family physician and the problem of suicide," by
B. H. Roisum. GP 33:87-93, March, 1966.

"M. D. suicides. Why?" by P. M. Margolis, MICH MED 67:
589, May, 1968.

"Occupational hazards to physicians --suicide," by H.
Freed. PENN MED 72:65-66, October, 1969.

"Physician's knowledge and attitudes about suicide,"
by D. A. Rockwell, et al. JAMA 225:1347-1349, September 10, 1973.

"The physician's role in suicide prevention," WHAT'S
NEW 214:16-17, Early Winter, 1959.

"Physicians who kill themselves," by K. D. Rose, et al.
ARCH GEN PSYCHIAT 29:800-805, December, 1973.

"Psychiatric illness in doctors," by R. M. Murray.
LANCET 1:211-213, JUne 15, 1974.

"The suicidal physician," by W. Simon. MINN MED 55:729-
732, August, 1972.

"Suicide among doctors," BRIT MED J 5386: 789-790, March
28, 1964.

"Suicide among physicians," by M. Ross. PSYCHIAT MED 2:
189-198, July, 1971.

"Suicide among physicians," by T. R. VanDellen. ILL
MED J 133:622, May, 1968.

"Suicide among physicians. A psychological study," by
M. Ross. DIS NERV SYST 34:145-150, March, 1973.

"Suicide among physicians/patients," by W. Simon, et al.
J NERV MENT DIS 147:105-112, August, 1968.

"Suicide and physician," by P. M. Kersten. J IOWA M SOC
45:610-614, December, 1955.

"Suicide and role strain among physicians," by D. E.
DeSole, et al. INT J SOC PSYCHIAT 15:294-301, Autumn,
1969.

"Suicide and the doctor-patient relationship," by H. M.
Perr. AM J PSYCHOANAL 28:177-188, 1968.

"Suicide and the family physician," by E. R. Inwood, et
al. GP 30:130-133, October, 1964.

"Suicide and the physician: experience and attitudes in
the community," by K. R. Whittemore, et al. J MED ASS
GA 61:307-311, September, 1972.

"Suicide by physicians," by P. H. Biachly, et al. BULL
SUICIDOL 2-18, December, 1968.

"Suicide by physicians," by A. G. Craig, et al. DIS NERV
SYST 29:763-772, November, 1968.

"Suicide by physicians," by D. C. Marcus. JAMA 229:141,
July 8, 1974.

"Suicide by physicians," by J. Mendlewicz, et al. AM J
PSYCHIAT 128:364-365, September, 1971.

"Suicide in physicians," by E. Cohen. JAMA 222:489,
October, 1972.

"The suicide problem: its growing importance for the
family physician," by H. T. Englehardt, et al. S MED
J 52:1536-1540, December, 1959.

"Suicides and the doctor," by N. S. Patel. PRACT 211:
197-201, August, 1973.

"Suicides by physicians in training," by J. C. Duffy.
J MED ED 43:1196, November, 1968.

PHYSICIANS: MALE VS. FEMALE SUICIDE RATE IN

PHYSICIANS: MALE VS. FEMALE SUICIDE RATE IN
  "Suicide in male and female physicians," by R. C. Step-
  pacher, et al. JAMA 228:323-328, April 15, 1974.

PHYSICIANS: OPTHAMOLOGISTS
  "Suicide and the opthamologist," by W. Bab.   EYE EAR
  NOSE THROAT MONTHLY 47:147-149, March, 1968.

PREDICTION: CHILDREN
  "How to spot the suicidal child," by D. Schuyler. AM
  SCH BD J 159:48, November, 1972.

  "Study probes youngsters' suicidal signs," TODAY'S
  HEALTH 47:82, April, 1969.

  "When was the last time you took a suicidal child to
  lunch?" by D. Schuyler. J SCH HEALTH 43:504-506,
  October, 1973.

PREDICTION: GENERAL
  "Affective states of patients immediately preceding
  suicide," by P. Keith-Spiegel, et al. J PSYCHIAT RES
  5:89-93, June, 1967.

  "Are you suicidal?" by M. Seligson.   HARP BAZ 105:62-
  63, August, 1972.

  "Assessment of suicidal risk by psychology and psychiatry trainees," by A. G. Burstein, et al. ARCH GEN PSY-
  CHIAT 29:792-793, December, 1973.

  "Attempt to employ a sentence completion test for the
  detection of psychiatric patients with suicidal ideas,"
  by H. Y. Efron.   J CONSULT PSYCHOL 24:156-160, April,
  1960.

  "Base rates in the prediction of suicide: a note on
  Applebaum's and Holzman's 'the color shading response
  and suicide'," by J. D. Pauker.   J PROJ TECHN 26:429-
  430, December, 1962.

  "Bender-Gestalt as an indicator of suicidal potential,"
  by C. V. Leonard.   PSYCHOL REP 32:665-666, April, 1973.

"Biochemical predictors of suicide," by G. Kreiger.
DIS NERV SYST 31:478-482, July, 1970.

"Can the potential suicide be recognized?" PULSE 17:12+,
#3, 1963.

"Characteristics of the suicide-prone," by G. M. Car-
stairs. PROC ROY SOC MED 54:262-264, April, 1961.

"Choosing to die: the decline of aggression and the rise
of suicide," by J. Binstock. FUTURIST 8:68-71, April,
1974.

"The complexity of motivations to suicidal attempts,"
by E. Stengel. J MENT SCI 106:1388-1393, October,
1960.

"Countertransference crisis in suicidal attempts," by
N. Tabachnick. ARCH GEN PSYCHIAT (CHICAGO) 4:572-
578, June, 1961.

"Danger periods for suicide in patients under treatment,"
by J. P. Copas, et al. PSYCHOL MED 1:400-404, November, 1971.

"Death ideation in suicidal patients," by S. Eisenthal.
J ABNORM PSYCHOL 73:162-167, April, 1968.

"Decision to die," by S. Alexander. LIFE 56:74-76+,
May 29, 1964.

"Definition of suicidal behaviors," by A. G. Devries.
PSYCHOL REP 22:1093-1098, June, 1968.

"Detection of suicidal patients: example of some limitations in the prediction of infrequent events," by A.
Rosen. J CONSULT PSYCHOL 18:397-403, December, 1954.

"Diagnosing 'suicidal risks' on Rorschach," by M. A.
White, et al. PSYCHIAT Q 26:161-189, 1952.

"Diagnosis of suicidal intent," by L. L. Havens. ANN
REV MED 20:419-424, 1969.

PREDICTION: GENERAL

"Divergencies between attitudes towards life and death among suicidal, psychosomatic, and normal hospitalized patients," by C. Neuringer.   J CONSULT CLIN PSYCHOL 32:59-63, February, 1968.

"Do they really want to die?" by K. B. Murphy.   TODAY'S HEALTH 43:48-49+, April, 1965.

"Dreams and suicide attempts," by D. L. Raphling.   J NERV MENT DIS 151:404-410, December, 1970.

"Durkheim's one cause of suicide," by B. D. Johnson. AM SOCIOL REV 30:875-876, December, 1965.

"The ecology of suicial behavior," by J. W. McCulloch, et al. BRIT J PSYCHIAT 113:313-319, March, 1967.

"Effects of foreknowledge of death in the assessment from case history material of intent to die," by R. W. Hood, Jr. J CONSULT CLIN PSYCHOL 34:129-133, April, 1970.

"Ethics of suicide," by T. S. Szasz. ANTIOCH R 31:7-17, Spring, 1971.

"Evaluating the suicidal risk," by A. Z. Schwartzberg. S MED 54:1017-1021, September, 1961.

"Events and conscious ideation leading to suicidal behavior in adolescence," by H. I. Schneer, et al. PSYCHIAT Q 35:507-515, July, 1961.

"Factors related to continued suicidal behavior in dyadic relationships," by Harris.   NR 15:72+, Winter, 1966.

"Forms of suicide and their significance," by J. Cohen. TRIANGLE 6:280-286, December, 1964.

"Further suicidal behavior: the development and validation of predictive scales," by D. Buglass, et al. BRIT J PSYCHIAT 116:483-491, May, 1970.

"The geriatric suicide," by J. Poulos. BED NURS 4:24-26, July, 1971.

"Half of suicides had given advance warning," SCI N L
74:89, August 9, 1958.

"How suicidal behaviors are learned," by C. J. Frederick, et al. AM J PSYCHOTHER 25:37-55, January, 1971.

"How to recognize the suicidal patient," by Rosenbaum.
RES PHYS 13:148+, April, 1967.

"I want out," by J. H. Pollack. TODAY'S HEALTH 49:32-
34+, January, 1971.

"Identifying suicide risk groups among attempted suicides," by J. Tuckman, et al. PUBLIC HEALTH REP 78:
763-766, September, 1963.

"Increase in suicidal thoughts and tendencies. Association with diazepam therapy," by H. F. Ryan, et al.
JAMA 203:1137-1139, March 25, 1968.

"An indicator of suicidal ideation on the Rorschach
Test," by A. Sapolsky. J PROJ TECHN 27:332-335,
September, 1963.

"An instrument for evaluating suicide potential: a preliminary study," by E. Cohen, et al. AM J PSYCHIAT
122:886-891, February, 1966.

"Is your patient considering suicide?" by Bennett. RN
25:71, June, 1962.

"Killers who never go to jail," by M. M. Hunt. SAT EVE
POST 226:24-25+, February 6, 1954.

"The kind of a person who may try it," by Alexander. RN
29:34+, March, 1966.

"Life sentence then suicide. The sad case of Richard
Holmes," by D. Blair. MED SCI LAW 11:162-179, October,
1971.

"Lifetime contract: technique for predicting suicides,"
by A. Wolff. SAT R WORLD 1:8, January 26, 1971.

"Manipulative suicide," by P. E. Sifneos. PSYCHIAT Q
40:525-537, July, 1966.

"The methods of suicide," by A. Capstick. MEDICOLEGAL
J 29:33-38, 1961.

"Model for the prediction of suicidal behavior," by A.
G. Devries. PSYCHOL REP 22:285-302, June, 1968.

"Multiple determinants of suicidal efforts," by L. S.
Kubie. J NERV MENT DIS 138:3-8, January, 1964.

"Multiple MMPI profiles of suicidal persons," by A. G.
Devries, et al. PSYCHOL REP 21:401-405, October, 1967.

"Multivariate analysis of clinical rating profiles of
suicidal psychiatric in-patients," by J. H. Patrick,
et al. J PROJ TECHN 33:138-145, April, 1969.

"New test helps make suicide predictable: index of
potential suicide," by W. Hartley, et al. SCI DIG
72:25-31+, November, 1972.

"A new experimental approach to the relationship between color-shading and suicide attemp-s," by D. B.
Colson, et al. J PERS ASSESS 37:237-241. June, 1973.

"On accidents and incidents: a study of self-destruction," by M. Rosenberg. COMPR PSYCHIAT 8:108-118,
April, 1967.

"On the love of suicide," by R. Winegarten. COMMENTARY
54:29-34, August, 1972.

"Options in suicidal crisis," by R. Steenland. NASPA J
10:328-332, April, 1973.

"Physicians can detect potential suicides says psychiatrist," TODAY'S HEALTH 46:14-15, February, 1968.

"Possibility of a biochemical test for suicidal potential:
an analysis of endrocrine findings prior to three suicides," by W. E. Bunny, et al. ARCH GEN PSYCHIAT
(CHICAGO) 13:232-239, September, 1965.

"The potentially suicidal patient," by D. H. Naftulin.
CA MED 111:169-176, September, 1969.

"The practical recognition of depressive and suicidal
states," by M. Ross. ANN INTERN MED 64:1079-1086,
May, 1966.

"Precursors of suicide," by Schneidman. MED INSIGHT 1:
40+, November, 1969.

"Predicting suicide of patients not practical," SCI N
L 67:205, March 26, 1955.

"Prediction of successful suicide from the Rorschach
test, using a sign approach," by P. G. Daston, et al.
J PROJECT TECHN 24:355-361, December, 1960.

"Psychiatrist examines suicide, questions and answers:
excerpts from Encyclopedia of Mental Health," by P.
Friedman. TODAY'S HEALTH 41:56-59+, December, 1963;
Correction. 42:87, January, 1961.

"Psychodynamic relationships: suicide and flying phobia,"
by P. F. Eggertsen. INT PSYCHIAT CLIN 4:155-175, Winter, 1967.

"Psychological autopsies of hospital suicides," by C.
Krieger. HOSP COMM PSYCHIAT 19:218-220, July, 1968.

"Psychotherapy designed to detect and treat suicidal
potential," by H. M. Schein, et al. AM J PSYCHIAT
125:1247-1251, March, 1969.

"Psychotherapy of suicidal patient," by L. M. Moss, et
al. AM J PSYCHIAT 112:814-820, April, 1956.

"Recognition of suicidal drives and tendencies in patients," by J. H. Wall. M REC & ANN 47:737, December,
1953.

"Recognition of suicidal risk: the physician's responsibility," by G. E. Murphy. S MED J 62:723-728, June,
1969.

"Recognition of suicidal risks through the psychologic
examination," by L. L. Havens. N E J MED 279:210-215,
January 26, 1967.

PREDICTION: GENERAL

"A reexamination of the color-shading Rohrschach test
response and suicide attempts," by S. A. Appelbaum,
et al. J PROJ TECHN 32:160164, April, 1968.

"Role of dread in suicidal behavior," by D. E. Spiegel,
et al. J ABNORM SOC PSYCHOL 66:507-511, May, 1963.

"The Rohrschach test as a research device for the identification, prediction, and understanding of suicidal
ideation and behavior," by C. Neuringer. J PROJ TECHN
29:71-82, March, 1965.

"Southern violence," by S. Hackney. AM HIST R 74:906-
925, February, 1969.

"Suicidal behavior in men and women," by D. Lester.
MENT HYG 53:340-345, July, 1969.

"The suicidal fit. A psychobiologic study on Puerto
Rican immigrants," by E. C. Trautman. ARCH GEN PSYCH-
IAT (CHICAGO) 5:76-83, July, 1961.

"The suicidal patient," by Stengel. NT 59:1083+, August,
30, 1963.

"Suicide -- a need for sympathy," bY G. H. Day. NT 67:
1235-1236, October 7, 1971.

"Suicide and dangerous sports: parachuting," by D. Lester, et al. JAMA 215:485, January 18, 1971.

"Suicide and ECT," by R. Abrams. AM J PSYCHIAT 126:272,
August, 1969.

"Suicide and suggestibility -- the role of the press,"
by J. A. Motto. AM J PSYCHIAT 124:252-256, August,
1967.

"Suicide and the doctor-patient relationship," by H. M.
Perr. AM J PSYCHOANAL 28 NO.2:187-188, 1968.

"Suicide and the psychiatrist," by M. Ross. AM J
PSYCHIAT 130:937, August, 1973.

"Suicide among chemists," by F. P. Li. ARCH ENVIRON
HEALTH (CHICAGO) 19:518-520, October, 1969.

"Suicide as seduction: a concept for evaluation of suicidal risk," by Blachly. HOSP MED 5:117+, September, 1969.

"Suicide: how you can spot a potential victim," by Murphy. EMERG MED 1:36+, April, 1969.

"Suicide patterns in the elderly," GERIAT 22:68, December, 1967.

"Suicide potential and time perspective," by R. I. Yufit, et al. ARCH GEN PSYCHIAT (CHICAGO) 23:158-163, August, 1970.

"The suicide six: observations on suicidal behavior and group function," by D. Reiss. INT J SOC PSYCHIAT 14: 201-212, Summer, 1968.

"Suicide, sleep, and death: some possible interrelations among cessation, interuption, and continuation phenomena," by E. S. Shneidman. J CONSULT PSYCHOL 28:95-106, April, 1964.

"Suicide: the patient's viewpoint," NT 61:1700, December 10, 1965.

"A syndrome of serious suicidal intent," by A. A. Stone. AMA ARCH GEN PSYCHIAT 3:331-339, October, 1960.

"Systems theory and self-destructive behavior: a new theoretical base," by K. P. Blaker. PERSPECT PSYCHIAT CARE 10:168-172, 1972.

"Theories of self-destruction," by N. Tabachnick. AM J PSYCHOANAL 32:53-61, 1972.

"Thinking of suicide?" by H. Thompson. AM MERC 77:125-127, December, 1953.

"Threats and meaning," NEWSWEEK 45:74, January 10, 1955.

"Use of Baye's Theorem in clinical decision. Suicidal risk, differential diagnosis, response to treatment," by J. Kraus. BRIT J PSYCHIAT 120:561-567, May, 1972.

PREDICTION: GENERAL

"Veterans and suicidal tendencies," NEW YORK TIMES 20:
3, May 8, 1953.

"Wanting to die -- case conference," by Brassington.
NT 62:1253+, September 23, 1966.

"Way of suicide," NEWSWEEK 71: 97, April 1, 1968.

"When suicide seems the only way out," by G. Day. FAM-
ILY HEALTH 3:34-35+, July, 1971.

"Why people can't take it," by F. R. Schreiber, et al.
SCI DIG 56:66-69, September, 1964.

"Whys of suicide," TIME 64:61, October 4, 1954.

"Will that patient commit suicide?" PT CARE 2:55+, October, 1968.

"With suicidal patients: caring for is caring about,"
by Umscheid. AJN 67:1230+, June, 1967.

PREVENTION: ADOLESCENTS
SEE ALSO: ADOLESCENCE
"Too young to die: help for teenagers by Rescue, Incorp-
orated: interview," ed. by R. W. O'Donnell, et al.
SR SCH 91:SUPP :7-8, November 16, 1967.

"When the cry comes for help: teen suicide and the Los
Angeles suicide prevention center," by J. M. Hoag.
SEVENTEEN   32:118-119+, March, 1973.

"Young people, suicide and the need for attention: work
of the Samaritans in Great Britain," PSYCHOL TODAY
7:88, March, 1974.

PREVENTION: GENERAL
"Action and reaction in suicidal crisis," by L. J. Mc-
Lean. NURS FORUM 8:28-41, 1969.

"Acutely suicidal patients. Management in general medical practice," by R. E. Litman. CA MED 104:168-174,
March, 1966.

"Alcohol in suicide and homicide," by D. W. Goodwin. Q J STUD ALCOHOL 34:144-156, March, 1973.

"Alternatives to the suicide prevention approach to mental health," by J. Hitchcock, et al. ARCH GEN PSYCHIAT (CHICAGO) 22:547-549, June, 1970.

"Answering cries for help," by T. Northcutt. J FLA MED ASS 51:301-302, May, 1964.

"The antisuicide pill," by D. Lester. JAMA 208:1908, June 9, 1969.

"Anti-suicide service in New Orleans," by W. C. Swanson. J LA STATE MED SOC 123:83-90, March, 1971.

"Attempted suicide," by Ralph. NT 63:688+, May 26, 1967.

"Attempted suicide presenting at the Alfred Hospital, Melbourne," by R. C. Buckle, et al. MED J AUST 1:754-758, May 22, 1965.

"Attempts to predict suicidal risk using psychological testing," by D. Lester. PSYCHOL BULL 74:1-17, July, 1970.

"Attitudes toward death held by staff of a suicide prevention center," by D. Lester. PSYCHOL REP 28:650, April, 1971.

"Avert imminent suicide: emergency centers," SCI N L 88:362, December 4, 1965.

"Bismarck's suicide prevention service," by L. A. Hoff. BULL SUICIDOLOGY 44:44-45, 1968.

"Blindspots in recognizing serious suicidal intentions," by H. Zee. BULL MENN CLIN 36:551-555, September, 1972.

"Broadening the focus of suicide prevention activities utilizing the public health model," by T. C. Welu, et al. AM J PUBLIC HEALTH 62:1625-1628, December, 1972.

"Broken homes and suicide," JAMA 191:494, February 8, 1965.

"Can the potential suicide be recognized?" PULSE 17: 12+, #3, 1963.

"Can we stop suicides?" by N. L. Farberow, et al TODAY'S HEALTH 41:59+, December, 1963.

"Cases of attempted suicide admitted to a general hospital," by J. A. Harrington, et al. BRIT MED J 5150: 463-467, September, 1959.

"Causes and prevention of repeated attempted suicide," by C. Bagley. SOC & ECON ADMIN 4:322-330, October, 1970.

"Chronic callers to a suicide prevention center," by D. Lester, et al. COMM MENT HEALTH J 6:246-250, June, 1970.

"The clients of the telephone samaritan service in Western Australia," by R. A. Finlay-Jones, et al. MED J AUST 1:690-694, April 1, 1972.

"The clinical assessment and management of the potential suicide," by I. F. Small, et al. J IND MED ASS 59: 1301-1306, November, 1966.

"Comments on the 'suicide prevention contribution to mental health', by D. Lester," by J. Hitchcock. PSYCHOL REP 28:986, June, 1971.

"A community anti-suicidal organization," by H. L. Resnik. CURR PSYCHIAT THER 4:253-259, 1964.

"A community's answer to the cry for help," by D. Hoxworth, et al. HOSP COMM PSYCHIAT 21:296-297, September, 1970.

"A comparison between 'Samaritan suicides' and living Samaritan clients," by B. M. Barraclough, et al. BRIT J PSYCHIAT 120:79-84, January, 1972.

"Comparison of accomplished suicides with persons contacting a crisis intervention clinic," by G. Greaves, et al. PSYCHOL REP 31:290, August, 1972.

"A computer interview for suicide-risk prediction," by
J. H. Greist, et al. AM J PSYCHIAT 130:1327-1332,
December, 1973.

"Control variables in the identification of suicidal
behavior," by A. G. Devries. PSYCHOL REP 20:SUPP:
1131-1135, June, 1967.

"A course on death education and suicide prevention:
implications for health education," by D. Leviton.
J AM COLL HEALTH ASS 19:217-220, April, 1971.

"Cries for help: Los Angeles suicide prevention center,"
TIME 80:60, August 17, 1962.

"Crisis maintenance," by K. Blaker. NURS FORUM 8:42-
49, 1969.

"The crisis treatment of suicide," by N. Tabachnick.
CA MED 112:1-8, June, 1970.

"A cry for help: suicide and accident proneness," by
McGuire. J PSYCHIAT NURS 2:500+, September-October,
1964.

"Depression and suicide reassessed," by C. M. Anderson.
J AM MED WOM ASS 19:467-471, June, 1964.

"Detection and management of the suicidal patient,"
by Mintz. DM 1961:3+, July,1961.

"Dial Mansion House 9000. The samaritans," by E. Anstice. NT 63:123-124, January 27, 1967.

"Distress behavior: a study of selected samaritan clients and parasuicides (attempted suicide patients),"
by N. Kreitman, et al. BRIT J PSYCHIAT 123:9-14,
July, 1973.

"Do not try to jolly suicidal person," SCI N L 78:93,
August 6, 1960.

"Doctors' wives tackle the suicide problem," by M. Benson. TODAY'S HEALTH 42:60-63, May, 1964.

"ED telephone: a lifeline for potential suicides,"
by H. L. Resnik, et al. RN 37:OR/ED 1-2+, October,
1974.

"Effect of suicide prevention centers on suicide rates
in the United States," by D. Lester. HEALTH SERV REP
89:37-39, January-February, 1974.

"The effectiveness of a suicide prevention program,"
by I. W. Weiner. MENT HYG 53:357-363, July, 1969.

"Emotional first aid," by F. H. Frankel. ARCH ENVIRON
HEALTH (CHICAGO) 11:824-827, December, 1965.

"Evaluation and management of suicide reactions," by
T. L. Dorpat. MED TIMES 91:1212-1218, December,
1963.

"The evaluation of a suicide prevention scheme by an
ecological method," by C. Bagley. SOC SCI MED 2: 1-
14, March, 1968.

"Experience in suicide prevention. 'Calls for help in
Chicago'," by J. L. Wilkins. ILL MED J 137:257-260,
March, 1970.

"The family physician and suicide prevention," by D. E.
Sanborn, 3rd., et al. AM FAM PHYS G P 1:75-78, March,
1970.

"A follow-up study of those who called a suicide prevention center," by J. Wilkins. AM J PSYCHIAT 127:
155-161, August, 1970.

"Guidelines for 'suicide-proofing' a psychiatric unit,"
by H. S. Berensohn, et al. AM J PSYCHOTHERAP 27:
204-212, April, 1973.

"Help for the despairing. The work of the Samaritans,"
by R. Fox. LANCET 2:1102-1105, November 24, 1962.

"Hopelessness, depression, and attempted suicide," by
K. Minkoff, et al. AM J PSYCHIAT 130:455-459, April,
1973.

"The hospital's obligation toward suicide-prone patients," by R. E. Litman, et al. HOSP 40:64-68, December 16, 1966.

"How the Samaritans combat suicide," by C. Varah. MENT HEALTH 21:132-134, October, 1962.

"How to keep patients from jumping out of the window," TRANS-ACTION 7:13, February, 1970.

"How to recognize the suicidal patient," by Rosenbaum. RES PHYS 13:148+, April, 1967.

"How to start a suicide prevention center without really trying," by B. L. Danto. MICH MED 69:119-121, February, 1970.

"I don't know why I'm calling, nobody can help me," by B. Asbell. REDBOOK 135:53+, June, 1970.

"I want to die: save me. Ambivalence: a theoretical aspect of a suicidal crisis," by K. Blaker. VA NURS Q 38:37-47, Summer, 1970.

"I'm going to kill myself," by A. Hamilton. SCI DIG 54: 57-63, September, 1963.

"Identifying suicide risk groups among attempted su- icides," by Tuckman, et al. PUB HEALTH REP (WASH) 78:763+, September, 1963.

"Identification of suicidal behavior by means of the MMPI," by A. G. Devries. PSYCHOL REP 19:415-419, October, 1966.

"An indicator of suicidal ideation on the Bender Visual Motor Gestalt Test," by D. Sternberg, et al. J PROJ TECHN 29:377-379, September, 1965.

"The kind of a person who may try it," by Alexander. RN 29:34+, March, 1966.

"The lethal impulse: climbing suicide toll spurs in- tensive study and prevention efforts," by W. S. Pink- erton, Jr. WALL ST J 173:1+, March 6, 1969.

"Letter: basic research and suicide prevention," by D. Lester. AM J PSYCHIAT 130:1402-1403, December, 1973.

"Letter: the prevention of suicide," by D. Lester. JAMA 228:26-27, April 1, 1974.

"Letter: suicide prevention centers: data from 1970," by D. Lester. JAMA 229:394, July 22, 1974.

"Letter: suicide prevention efforts," by D. Lester. JAMA 227:77-78, January 7, 1974.

"Life you can save," by C. P. Weikel. HAR YRS 10:6-11, January, 1970.

"Lifetime contract: technique for preventing suicides," by A. Wolff. SAT R WORLD 1:8, January 26, 1974.

"Lifeline for would-be suicides: with list of suicide prevention centers," by J. N. Bell. TODAY'S HEALTH 45:30-33+, June, 1967.

"Lord Jesus will answer: telephone help for the discouraged," TIME 57:69, February 12, 1951.

"The Los Angeles suicide prevention center," NO 13:61, November, 1965.

"Los Angeles suicide prevention center," by R. E. Litman, et al. AM J PSYCHIAT 117:1084-1087, June, 1961.

"The Los Angeles suicide prevention center: a demonstration of public health feasibilities," by E. S. Shneidman, et al. AM J PUB HEALTH 55:21-26, January, 1965.

"Management and prognosis of suicidal attempts in old age," by I. R. C. Batchelor. GERIAT 10:291-293, June, 1955.

"The management of self-destructive patients," by H. Graff. AM J PSYCHIAT 126:1041-1042, January, 1970.

"Management of suicide attempt," by J. L. Denner. NY J MED 70:1666-1667, June 15, 1970.

"Market analysis for suicide prevention. Relationship of age to suicide on holidays, day of the week and month," by P. H. Blachly, et al. NORTHWEST MED 68: 232-238, March, 1969.

"A matter of life and death. A report on a national center for suicidologists," by Coogan. SKF PSYCHIAT REP 37:21+, March-April, 1968.

"Means of preventing suicides," NEW YORK TIMES 60:1, September 26, 1971.

"Medical management of suicide victim," by I. S. Friedman. NY J MED 66:3007-3009, December 1, 1966.

"Method stops suicide in military service," SCI N L 69: 296, May 12, 1956.

"Moon phases, suicide, and homicide," by A. D. Pokorny. AM J PSYCHIAT 121:66-67, July, 1964.

"The mystical experience as a suicide preventive," by P. C. Horton. AM J PSYCHIAT 130:294-296, March, 1973.

"The myth of suicide prevention," by D. Lester. COMPR PSYCHIAT 13:555-560, November-December, 1972.

"National suicide prevention center planned," NEW YORK TIMES 63:1, October 15, 1965.

"New direction for suicide prevention centers," by A. Kiev. AM J PSYCHIAT 127:87-88, July, 1970.

"A new way to rescue suicides: new preventive centres in Europe and the U.S. with 24-hour stand-by teams of specialists ready to help offer a pattern for action," by B. Rose. MACLEAN'S 78:20+, October 2, 1965.

"Non-professional experts," by Coogan. SKF PSYCHIAT REP 43:7+, Spring, 1969.

"A note on the group management of a disgruntled suicidal patient," by E. R. Miller, et al. INT J GROUP PSYCHOTHERAP 13:216-218, April, 1963.

"The nurse in suicide prevention," by M. A. Wallace.
NURS OUTLOOK 14:55-57, March, 1967.

"The nurse's role in the prevention of suicide," by
Farberow, et al. NURS FORUM 3:92+, #1, 1964.

"On assessing the theory of status integration and suicide," by J. P. Gibbs, et al. AM SOC REV 31:533-541,
August, 1966.

"Options in suicidal crisis," by R. Steenland. NASPA J
10:328-332, April, 1973.

"Organization of a suicide prevention center," by H. H.
Brunt, Jr. J MED SOC NJ 66:62-65, February, 1969.

"An organizational study of suicide prevention agencies
in the United States," by A. R. Roberts. POLICE 14:
64-72, May/June, 1970.

"Organizing and funding suicide prevention and crisis
services," by C. J. Frederick. HOSP COMM PSYCHIAT 23:
346-348, November, 1972.

"Physicians can detect potential suicides, says psychiatrist," TODAY'S HEALTH 46:14-15, February, 1968.

"Physician's responsibility for suicide prevention,"
J MED SOC NJ 64:101-102, March, 1967.

"Physician's responsibility in prevention," by A. Bennett. DIS NERV SYST 15:207-210, July, 1954.

"A plan for preventing student suicide," by D. E. Berg.
SCH HEALTH REV 1:6-11, September, 1970.

"Precautions and responsibilities in handling patient
suicides," by C. U. Letourneau. HOSP 27:80-88,
January, 1953.

"Prediction and prevention of suicide," CAN MED ASS J
100:867-868, May 10, 1969.

"Premenstrual symptoms in self-referrals to a suicide prevention service," by R. D. Wetzel, et al. BRIT J PSYCHIAT 119:525-526, November, 1971.

"The presuicidal patient: recognition and management," by M. Ross. S MED J 60:1094-1098, October, 1967.

"The present state of suicide prevention -- an African survey," by S. G. Bloomberg. INT J SOC PSYCHIAT 18:104-108, Summer, 1972.

"Preventing suicide," by Shneidman. AJN 65:111+, May, 1965.

"Preventing suicides," S THOMAS NURS J 5:364+, March, 1967.

"Prevention of suicide," by A. N. Avella. NY J MED 66: 3023-3025, December 1, 1966.

"Prevention of suicide," by A. E. Bennett. POSTGRAD MED 32:160-164, August, 1962.

"The prevention of suicide," by A. E. Bennett CA MED 81:396-401, December, 1954.

"Prevention of suicide," BRIT MED J 1:419, February 20, 1971.

"The prevention of suicide," by E. D. Cunningham. MED J AUST 48(1):46-49, January 14, 1961.

"Prevention of suicide," by T. E. Dancey. CAN NURS 62: 29-32, February, 1966.

"Prevention of suicide," by D. Lester. JAMA 225-992, August 20, 1973.

"The prevention of suicide," by R. E. Litman. CURR PSYCH-IAT THER 6:268-276, 1966.

"Prevention of suicide,: WHO PUBLIC HEALTH PAP 35:1-84, 1968.

"Prevention of suicide as a public health problem," by J. R. Oliven. AM J PUB HEALTH 44:1419-1425, November, 1954.

"Procedures used in crisis intervention by suicide prevention agencies," by A. R. Roberts, et al. PUBLIC HEALTH REP 85:691-697, August, 1970.

"Producing suicides," by J. L. Wilkins. AM BEHAV SCI 14:185-201, November, 1970.

"Psychiatric hospitals and suicide prevention centers," by R. E. Litman. COMPR PSYCHIAT 6:119-127, April, 1965.

"Psychiatry and suicide: the management of a mistake," by D. W. Light, Jr. AM J SOC 77:821-838, March, 1972.

"Quiet cries. Can I help you? Will you listen?" by M. Heath. NURS CARE 6:26-30, April, 1973.

"Reaching hands, a plunge to death," LIFE 32:31, March 10, 1952.

"Reading the signals for suicide risk," by R. Niccolini. GERIAT 28:71-72, May, 1973.

"Recognition of the suicidal patient," by B. S. Merseau. MED BULL US ARMY EUROPE 16:188-190, September, 1959.

"Recognizing the potential suicide," by A. E. Bennett. GERIAT 22:175-181, May, 1967.

"Recognizing the suicidal patient," by B. R. Shochet. MD MED J 18:65-67, September, 1969.

"Reducing the toll of suicide," PULSE 17:15+, #3, 1963.

"Replicability of Rohrschach signs with known degrees of suicidal intent," by F. Cutter, et al. J PROJ TECHN 32:428-434, October, 1968.

"Report on the crisis intervention and suicide prevention centre for Greater Vancouver," by B. Tarrant. CAN J PUB HEALTH 61:66-67, January-February, 1970.

"Rescue, inc.," by Davis. HOSP TOP 41:42+, May, 1963.

"Rescue, incorporated," AMERICA 116:6, January 7, 1967.

"Rescue, inc. and the licensed practical nurse," by K. B. Murphy. AM J PRACT NURS 2:32-34, January, 1966.

"The rescue system," by L. J. McClean. PER PSYCHIAT CARE 10:173-177, 1972.

"The role of the physician in suicide prevention," by R. L. Garrard. N C MED J 30:473-476, December, 1969.

"Shall we prevent suicide?" by R. Noyes, Jr. COMPR PSYCHIAT 11:361-370, July, 1970.

"Show versus no show: a comparison of referral calls to a suicide prevention and crisis service," by K. Slaikeu, et al. J CONSULT CLIN PSYCHOL 40:481-486, June, 1973.

"Social and medical responsibility in suicide prevention," by C. I. Wold. WIS MED J 66:535-539, November, 1967.

"Sociology of suicide prevention: policy implications of differences between suicidal patients and completed suicides," by R. W. Maris. SOC PROB 17:132-149, Summer, 1969.

"Some clinical considerations in the prevention of suicide based on a study of 134 successful suicides," by E. Robins, et al. AM J PUBLIC HEALTH 49:898-899, July, 1959.

"Some considerations in establishing a suicide prevention service: Ventura County suicide prevention service," by R. T. Jarmusz. MENT HYG 53:351-356, July, 1969.

"Some practical procedures in the management of suicidal persons," by R. S. Mintz. AM J ORTHOPSYCHIAT 36:896-903, October, 1966.

"Special issue commemorating the tenth anniversary of the Los Angeles suicide prevention center," by E. Shneidman. BULL SUICIDOL 1-65, Spring, 1970.

"Special report on a growing social problem: when the
cry for help comes: suicide prevention centers," by
J. N. Bell. GOOD H 162:108-109+, June, 1966.

"Special 24-hour phone service to curb suicides," NEW
YORK TIMES 8:4, August 28, 2963.

"Suicidal behavior and external constraints," by D.
Lester. PSYCHOL REP 27:777-778, December, 1970.

"Suicidal configurations in the Bender-Gestalt," by
M. M. Nawas, et al. J PROJ TECHN 32:392-394, August,
1968.

"Suicidal depression and physical illness," by J. Fawcett. JAMA 219:1303-1306, March 6, 1972.

"Suicidal impulse in depression and paranoia," by T.
E. Allen. INT J PSYCHOANAL 48:433-438, 1967.

"The suicidal patient," by I. W. Sletten, et al. MO MED
69:864-867, November, 1972.

"The suicidal patient. Some considerations in evaluation and management," by S. Soreff. J MAINE MED ASS
63:225-226, October, 1972.

"Suicidal precautions: a dilemma in the therapeutic
community," by P. M. Margolis, et al. ARCH GEN PSYCH-
IAT (CHICAGO) 13:224-231, September, 1965.

"Suicide: a new attack against an old killer," by J.
Star. LOOK 30:60+, August 23, 1966.

"Suicide after contact with a suicide prevention center,"
by C. I. Wold, et al. ARCH GEN PSYCHIAT 28:735-739,
May, 1973.

"Suicide among us: can we learn to prevent it?" by C.
B. Thomas. JOHNS HOPKINS MED J 125:276-285, November,
1969.

"Suicide and how to prevent it," by M. O. Vincent. CHR
TODAY 14:10-12, January 16, 1970.

"Suicide and its prevention," WHO CHRON 22:489-491, November, 1968.

"Suicide and overcontrol," by D. Lester, et al. PSYCHOL REP 32:1278, June, 1973.

"Suicide and suicide prevention: a legal analysis," by R. E. Schulman. AM BAR ASS J 54:855-862, September, 1968.

"Suicide and suicide prevention: an overview," by A. R. Roberts. PUBLIC HEALTH REVS 2:3-30, February, 1973.

"Suicide and the hospital service: a study of hospital records of patients who subsequently committed suicide," by K. Jones. BRIT J PSYCHIAT 111:625-630, July, 1965.

"Suicide can't be eliminated," by A. Herzog. NEW YORK TIMES MAG 32-33+, March 20, 1966.

"Suicide-- causes and prevention: statistics and public health significance," by P. I. Robinson. POSTGRAD MED 32:154-159, August, 1962.

"Suicide consultation: a psychiatric service to social agencies," by M. N. Kaplan, et al. AM J PSYCHIAT 122: 1357-1361, June, 1966.

"Suicide:demography of suicide: methods and fashions: dynamics predictability and prevention: the trouble shooting clinic," by J. Hirsh. MENT HYG 43:516-525, October, 1959; 44:3-11, January, 1960; 274-280, April, 1960; 382-389, July, 1960, 496-502, October, 1960.

"Suicide: dynamics, incidence, detection, and prevention," by B. G. Pineda. J PHILLIPP FED PRIV MED PRACT 13: 474-481, July, 1964.

"Suicide: guide lines for handling patient," by Humiston. EMERG MED 1:38+, April, 1969.

"Suicide: motivation and prevention," by R. Noyes, Jr. POSTGRAD MED, 47:182-187, March, 1970.

PREVENTION: GENERAL

"Suicide: need for a significant other," by E. T.
Culver. CHR CENT 86:100-102, January 15, 1969.

"Suicide. Part 4. Predictibility and prevention," by
J. Hirsch. MENT HYG 44:382-389, July, 1960.

"Suicide prevention," BRIT MED J 4:513-514, November 29,
1969.

"Suicide prevention," by B. M. Barraclough, et al.
LANCET 2:365, August 15, 1970.

"Suicide prevention: a myth or a mandate?" by C. Bagley.
BRIT J PSYCHIAT 123:130, July, 1973.

"Suicide prevention: a myth or a mandate?" by A. Malle-
son. BRIT J PSYCHIAT 122:238-239, February, 1973.

"Suicide prevention. A study of the community program
in Kansas City," by R. E. Bidwell, et al. J KANS MED
SOC 72:167-173, April, 1971.

"Suicide prevention: Adlerian contribution," by M. H.
Messer. J INDIV PSYCHOL 29:54-71, May, 1973.

"Suicide prevention and niacin," by H. L. Resnik. JAMA
208:2164, June 16, 1969.

"Suicide prevention and social clubs," by F. F. Wagner.
INT J SOC PSYCHIAT 11:116-117, Spring, 1965.

"Suicide prevention around the clock," by N. L. Farberow,
et al. AM J ORTHOPSYCHIAT 36:551-558, April, 1966.

"Suicide prevention as a public health problem," by F.
Oliven. AM J PUBLIC HEALTH 44:1419-1425, November,
1954.

"A suicide prevention center," by R. E. Litman, et al.
CURR PSYCHIAT THER 1:8-16, 1961.

"Suicide prevention center in a public mental hospital,"
by H. H. Braunt, et al. MENT HYG 52:254-262, April,
1968.

"A suicide prevention center in Vancouver," by B. Tarrant. CAN MENT HEALTH 18:11-14, May/August, 1970.

"A suicide prevention center on an indian reservation," by J. H. Shore, et al. AM J PSYCHIAT 128:1086-1091, March, 1972.

"A suicide prevention center in chicago," by F. M. Parks, et al. ILL MED J 133:306-310, March, 1968.

"The suicide prevention center in Los Angeles," by M. L. Peck. SCH HEALTH REV 1:31-33, September, 1970.

"Suicide prevention centers: comparisons of clients in several cities," by J. Wilkins. COMPR PSYCHIAT 10: 443-451, November, 1969.

"Suicide prevention clinic opened," NEW YORK TIMES 61: 3, March 28, 1971.

"The suicide prevention contribution to mental health," by D. Lester. PSYCHOL REP 28:903-905, June, 1971.

"Suicide prevention in Alaska," by L. Pilifant, et al. ALASKA MED 14:41-42, April, 1972.

"Suicide prevention in the nation's capital," by E. C. Noel, 3rd. MED ANN DC 40:526, August, 1971.

"Suicide prevention: NIMH wants more attention for taboo subject," by B. Nelson. SCIENCE 161:766-767, August 23, 1968.

"Suicide prevention on psychiatric wards," by Bennett, et al. MENT HOSP 16:105+, March, 1965.

"Suicide prevention programs and mental health associa- tions," by R. K. McGee. MENT HYG 55:60-67, January, 1971.

"Suicide prevention programs-- the current scene," by A. B. Haughton. AM J PSYCHIAT 124:1692-1696, June, 1968.

"Suicide prevention.   Review and evaluation," by A. N. Singh, et al. CAN PSYCHIAT ASS J 18:117-121, April, 1973.

"A suicide prevention schedule for neuro-psychiatric patients," by N. L. Farberow, et al. J NERV MENT DIS 158:408-419, June, 1974.

"Suicide prevention telephone service," by R. E. Litman, et al. JAMA 192:21-25, April 5, 1965.

"Suicide prevention.   The hospital's role," by Shneidman.   HOSP PRACT 3:56+, September, 1968.

"Suicide prevention -- the physician's role," by L. F. Saylor.   CA MED 112:102-103, March, 1970.

"Suicide stoppers," by R. Miller.   CORONET 46:108-112, September, 1959.

"Suicides anonymous," TIME 66:57, October 17, 1955.

"Therapy treatments for preventing suicides," NEW YORK TIMES 17:1, September 29, 1968.

"The trouble shooting clinic: prototype of a comprehensive community emergency service," by J. Hirsh.   MENT HYG 44:496-502, October, 1960.

"Toward suicide prevention in medical practice," by J. A. Motto.   JAMA 210:1229-1232, November 17, 1969.

"Treating suicide: the illusions of a professional movement," by D. W. Light, Jr., INT SOC SCI J 25, #4:475, 488, 1973.

"Treatment of the suicidal patient: community psychiatry approach," by A. L. Seale, et al. S MED J 58:1159-1162, September, 1965.

"Upsurge in suicides and ways to prevent them," US NEWS 77:17-18, July 1, 1971.

"Urban problems and suicide prevention," by H. L. Resnik. AM J PSYCHIAT 125:1723-1724, June, 1969.

PREVENTION: GENERAL

"When a patient threatens suicide," by M. K. Bodie. PERS
PSYCHIAT CARE 6:76-79, 1968.

"When listening means life: the samaritans and other suicide prevention groups," by R. J. Levin.   SAT R 49:
65, October 1, 1966.

"When the cry for help comes: teen suicide and the Los
Angeles suicide prevention center," by J. M. Hoag.
SEVENTEEN 32:118-119+, March, 1973.

"When you must act to block suicide," by Solomon. CON-
SULTANT 3:14+, November-December, 1963.

"With suicidal patients: caring for is caring about,"
by T. Umscheid.   AJN 67:1230-1232, June, 1967.

PREVENTION: SAMARITANS
"How the Samaritans combat suicide," by C. Varah.   MENT
HEALTH 21:132-134, October, 1962.

"The Samaritans," by M. N. Cowie.   DIST NURS 10:33, May,
1967.

"The Samaritans: a nurse's impressions," NURS MIRROR
134:26-27, March 31, 1-72.

"The Samaritans and the elderly: some problems in communication between a suicide prevention scheme and a
group with a high suicide rate," by M. Atkinson. SOC
SCI MED 5:483-490, October, 1971.

"Samaritans group formed to prevent suicides: founder
Rev. E. C. Varah comments," NEW YORK TIMES 9:2, November 23, 1957.

"The Samaritans -- help for the hopeless," NT 59:548+,
May 3, 1963.

"Suicide and Samaritan clients," by S. M. Barlow. LANCET
2:1091, November 21, 1970.

"Suicide and Samaritan clients," by B. M. Barraclough,
et al. LANCET 2:868-870, October 24, 1970.

PREVENTION: SUICIDE PREVENTION CENTERS

"Anti-suicide service in New Orleans," by W. C. Swanson. J LA STATE MED SOC 123:83-90, March, 1971.

"Attitudes toward death held by staff of a suicide prevention center," by D. Lester. PSYCHOL REP 28:650, April, 1971.

"Avert imminent suicide: emergency centers," SCI N L 88: 362, December 4, 1965.

"Bismarck's suicide prevention service," by L. A. Hoff. BULL SUICIDOL 44:44-45, 1968.

"Chronic callers to a suicide prevention center," by D. Lester, et al. COMM MENT HEALTH J 6:246-250, June, 1970.

"A community anti-suicidal organization," by H. L. Resnik. CURR PSYCHIAT THER 4:253-259, 1964.

"Comparison of accomplished suicides with persons contacting a crisis intervention clinic," by G. Greaves, et al. PSYCHOL REP 31:290, August, 1972.

"Cries for help: Los Angeles suicide prevention center," TIME 80:60, August 17, 1962.

"Dial Mansion House 9000. The samaritans," by E. Anstice. NT 63:123-124, January 27, 1967.

"Effect of suicide prevention centers on suicide rates in the United States," by D. Lester. HEALTH SERV REP 89:37-39, January-February, 1974.

"The effectiveness of a suicide prevention program," by I. W. Weiner. MENT HYG 53:357-363, July, 1969.

"Experience in suicide prevention. 'Calls for help in Chicago'," by J. L. Wilkins. ILL MED J 137:257-260, March, 1970.

"A follow-up study of those who called a suicide prevention center," by J. Wilkins. AM J PSYCHIAT 127: 155-161, August, 1970.

"How to start a suicide prevention center without really trying," by B. L. Danto. MICH MED 69:119-121, February, 1970.

"Letter: suicide prevention centers: data from 1970," by D. Lester. JAMA 229:394, July 22, 1974.

"Lifeline for would-be suicides: with list of suicide prevention centers," by J. N. Bell. TODAY'S HEALTH 45:30-33+, June, 1967.

"The Los Angeles suicide prevention center," NO 13:61, November, 1965.

"Los Angeles suicide prevention center," by R. E. Litman, et al. AM J PSYCHIAT 117:1084-1087, June, 1961.

"The Los Angeles suicide prevention center: a demonstration of public health feasibilities," by E. S. Shneidman, et al. AM J PUBLIC HEALTH 55:21-26, January, 1965.

"National suicide prevention center planned," NEW YORK TIMES 63:1, October 15, 1965.

"New direction for suicide prevention centers," by A. Kiev. AM J PSYCHIAT 127:87-88, July, 1970.

"A new way to rescue suicides: new p-eventive centers in Europe and the U. S. with 24-hour stand-by teams of specialists ready to help offer a pattern for action," by B. Rose. MACLEAN'S 78:20+, October 2, 1965.

"Organization of a suicide prevention center," by H. H. Brunt, Jr. J MED SOC NJ 66:62-65, February, 1969.

"An organization study of suicide prevention agencies in the United States," by A. R. Roberts. POLICE 14: 64-72, May/June, 1970.

"Organizing and funding suicide prevention and crisis services," by C. J. Frederick. HOSP COMMUN PSYCHIAT 23: 346-348, November, 1972.

"Procedures used in crisis intervention by suicide prevention agencies," by A. R. Roberts, et al. PUBLIC
HEALTH REP 85:691-697.

"Psychiatric hospitals and suicide prevention centers,"
by R. E. Litman. COMPR PSYCHIAT 6:119-127, April,
1965.

"Report on the crisis intervention and suicide prevention centre for Greater Vancouver," by B. Tarrant.
CAN J PUB HEALTH 61:66-67, January-February, 1970.

"Rescue, Inc., by Davis. HOSP TOP 41:42+, May, 1963.

"Rescue, Incorporated," AMERICA 116:6, January 7, 1967.

"Rescue, Incorporated and the licensed practical nurse,"
by K. B. Murphy. AM J PRACT NURS 2:32-34, January,
1966.

"Show versus no-show: a comparison of referral calls to
a suicide prevention and crisis center," by K. Slaikeu,
et al. J CONSULT CLIN PSYCHOL 40:481-486, June, 1973.

"Some considerations in establishing a suicide prevention service: Ventura County suicide prevention service," by R. T. Jarmusz. MENT HYG 53:351-356, July,
1969.

"Special issue commemorating the tenth anniversary of
the Los Angeles suicide prevention center," by E.
Shneidman. BULL SUICIDOL 1-65, Spring, 1970.

"Special report on a growing social problem: when the
cry for help comes: suicide prevention centers," by
J. N. Bell. GOOD H 162:108-109+, JUne, 1966.

"Suicide after contact with a suicide prevention center,"
by C. I. Wold, et al. ARCH GEN PSYCHIAT 28:735-739,
May, 1973.

"Suicide prevention. A study of the community program
in Kansas City," by R. E. Bidwell, et al. J KANS MED
SOC 72:167-173, April, 1971.

PREVENTION: SUICIDE PREVENTION CENTERS

"A suicide prevention center," by R. E. Litman, et al.
CURR PSYCHIAT THER 1:8-16, 1961.

"Suicide prevention center in a public mental hospital,"
by H. H. Braunt, et al. MENT HYG 52:254-262, April,
1968.

"A suicide prevention center in Vancouver," by B. Tarrant.
CAN MENT HEALTH 18:11-14, May/August, 1970.

"A suicide prevention center on an Indian reservation,"
by J. H. Shore, et al. AM J PSYCHIAT 128:1086-1091,
March, 1972.

"A suicide prevention center in Chicago," by F. M. Parks,
et al. ILL MED J 133:306-310, March, 1968.

"The suicide prevention center in Los Angeles," by M.
L. Peck. SCH HEALTH REV 1:31-33, September, 1970.

"Suicide prevention centers: comparisons of clients in
several cities," by J. Wilkins. COMPR PSYCHIAT 10:
443-451, November, 1969.

"Suicide prevention clinic opened," NEW YORK TIMES 61:
3, March 28, 1971.

"The trouble shooting clinic: prototype of a comprehensive community emergency service," by J. Hirsh. MENT
HYG 44:496-502, October, 1960.

"When listening means life: the samaritans and other suicide prevention groups," by R. J. Levin. SAT R 49:
65, October 1, 1966.

"When the cry for help comes: teen suicide and the Los
Angeles suicide prevention center," by J. M. Hoag.
SEVENTEEN 32:118-119+, March, 1973.

PREVENTION: TELEPHONE SERVICES
SEE TELEPHONE

PSYCHIATRISTS
"The creativity and suicide of a psychoanalyst," by V. Tausk, et al. PSYCHOANAL Q 41:556-584, 1972.

"Heal thyself: suicides among psychiatrists," NEWSWEEK 69:112, May 22, 1967.

"The psychiatrist and apparently imminent suicide," by S. Hirsch, et al. CAN PSYCHIAT ASS J 18:107-111, April, 1973.

"Psychiatrists who kill themsleves," by J. A. Winn. AM J PSYCHIAT 124:1270, March, 1968.

"Psychiatrists who kill themselves: a study in suicide," by W. Freeman. AM J PSYCHIAT 124:846-847, December, 1967.

"Psychiatrists who kill themselves: uncertainty of sources," by J. W. Goppelt. AM J PSYCHIAT 124:1471, April, 1968.

"Suicide in psychiatrists," by M. Braun. JAMA 223:81, January 1, 1973.

"Suicide rates among psychiatrists," by D. H. Rosen. JAMA 224:246-247, April 9, 1973.

PSYCHIATRY
"Advances in psychiatry," by R. Mitchell. NT 70:1085-1086+, July 11, 1974.

"Alternative to suicide," TIME 97:48, April 26, 1971.

"Behavioral sciences," SCI N 9:356, April 12, 1969.

"Bondage and suicide," by R. E. Litman, et al. ARCH GEN 27:80-85, July, 1972.

"A case of alcoholism and psychoneurotic depression, by Day. NM 127:39+, September 6, 1968.

"Comparative psychiatric study of accidental and suicidal death," by N. Tabachnick, et al. ARCH GEN PSYCHIAT (CHICAGO) 14:60-68, January, 1966.

"Culture and mental disorder: a study of attempted suicide," by E. Robins, et al. HUMAN ORGAN 16:7-11, Winter, 1958.

"Depression and suicidality," by C. V. Leonard. J CONSULT CLIN PSYCHOL 42:98-104, February, 1974.

"Depression and suicide -- treatment and prevention," by W. M. Mendel. CONSULTANT 12:115-116, January, 1962.

"Depression -- the mental cold," by M. Frost. NM 137: 46-47, October 5, 1973.

"Deviance, interpersonal relations and suicide," by W. A. Rushing. HUM REL 22:61-76, February, 1969.

"The effect of two simultaneous cognitive and affective stimuli on a group of chronic schizophrenic patients with suicidal ideation," by E. Starer. J CLIN PSYCHOL 16:341-343, July, 1960.

"Emotional reactions to death and suicide," by J. H. Masserman. AM PRACT & DIG TREAT 5:41-46, November, 1954.

"Epidemiology of depression: a review," by C. Silverman. AM J PSYCHIAT 124:890-891, January, 1968.

"Fear of death of suicidal persons," by D. Lester. PSYCHOL REP 20:SUPP: 1077-1078, June, 1967.

"Group psychotherapy with suicidal persons: a comparison with standard group method," by C. J. Frederick, et al. INT J SOC PSYCHIAT 16:103-111, Spring, 1970.

"How to cure depression," by F. R. Schreiber, et al. SCI DIG 61:12-15, February, 1967.

"Hysteria and suicide," by D. Lester. JAMA 224:902, May 7, 1973.

"An index of unnecessary deaths," by L. Guralnick, et al. PUBLIC HEALTH REP 82:180-182, February, 1967.

"Let's talk sense about suicide," by Clark. RN 23:58-62+, November, 1960.

"Melancholy and suicide," by E. Cohen. JAMA 212:2121, June 22, 1970.

"Mental illness and suicide," by R. W. Parnell. TIMES ED SUPP 1979:303, April 3, 1953.

"Misunderstood matter of suicide," by J. Horn. PSYCHOL TODAY 8:128, December, 1974.

"Monitoring and treatment of suicidal potential within the context of ps-chotherapy," by H. M. Shein, et al. COMPR PSYCHIAT 10:59-70, January, 1969.

"Neuroticism, extraversion and repression -- sensitization in suicidal college students," by C. E. Colson. BRIT J SOC CLIN PSYCHOL 11:88-89, February, 1972.

"Personality and the nature of suicidal attempts," by V. N. Murthy. BRIT J PSYCHIAT 115:791-795, July, 1969.

"Personality characteristics of attempted suicide," by K. S. Vinoda. BRIT J PSYCHIAT 112:1143-1150, November, 1966.

"The problem solving aspect of suicide," by S. A. Appelbaum. J PROJ TECHN 27:259-268, September, 1963.

"Psychiatric emergencies in general practice," by E. W. Anderson. PRACT 168:363-367, April, 1952.

"Psychiatric, physiological, behavioral and self-report measures in relation to a suicide attempt," by S. R. Platman, et al. J PSYCHIAT RES 8:127-137, June, 1971.

"A psychiatrist examines suicide," by Friedman. TODAY'S HEALTH 41:56+, December, 1963.

"Psychobiological characteristics in youth as predictors of five disease states: suicide, mental illness, hypretension, coronary heart disease and tumor," by C. B. Thomas, et al. JOHN HOPKINS MED J 132:16-43, January, 1973.

"Psychodynamics of depression and suicide," PULSE 17:6+, #3, 1963.

"The psychology and care of the maintenance hemodialysis patient," by N. B. Levy. HEART LUNG 2:400-405, May-June, 1973.

"Psychopathic states and attempted suicide," by I. R. C. Batchelor. BRIT MED J 1:1342-1347, June 12, 1954.

"Punishment experiences and suicidal preoccupation," by D. Lester. J GENET PSYCHOL 113:89-94, September, 1968.

"Reactions of a psychotherapy group to ambiguous circumstances surrounding the death of a group member," by D. D. Kirtley, et al. J CONSULT CLIN PSYCHOL 33:195-199, April, 1969.

"Reactions to interpersonal crisis in suicidal individuals," by C. Neuringer. J GEN PSYCHOL 71:47-55, July, 1964.

"Reflections of a psychiatrist," by Kramer. PROF NURS HOME 9:15+, August, 1967.

"The relationship between attempted suicide, depression and parent death," by J. Birtchnell. BRIT J PSYCHIAT 116:307-313, March, 1970.

"Resentment and dependency in the suicidal individual," by D. Lester. J GEN PSYCHOL 81:137-145, July, 1969.

"A retrospective examination of psychiatric case records of patients who subsequently committed suicide," by R. A. Flood, et al. BRIT J PSYCHIAT 114:43-50, April, 1968.

"Rigid thinking in suicidal individuals," by C. Neuringer. J CONSULT PSYCHOL 28:54-58, February, 1964.

"The role of psychotherapy in the treatment of suicidal persons: on the dramatization of death," by E. S. Shneidman. AM J PSYCHOTHER 25:4-17, January, 1971.

"Self-destructive and suicidal behaviors in a neuropsychiatric impatient facility," by J. J. Fabian, et al. AM J PSYCHIAT 130:1383-1385, December, 1973.

"Self-evaluation and subjective life expectancy among suicidal and nonsuicidal psychotic males," by S. Farnham-Diggory. J ABNORM SOC PSYCHOL 69:628-634, December, 1964.

"A study on the factors contributing to suicide from the standpoint of psychiatry," by K. Ohara. AM J PSYCHIAT 120:798-799, February, 1964.

"Special psychiatric problems of paraplegis: case of attempted suicide," by J. Petrus, et al. AM J PSYCHIAT 109:693-695, March, 1953.

"Subsequent suicide in depressed in-patients," by A. W. McDowell, et al. BRIT J PSYCHIAT 114:749-754, June, 1968.

"Suicidal behavior in men and women," by D. Lester. MENT HYG 53:340-345, July, 1969.

"The suicidal patient -- an inside view -- V. A. Wadsworth Hospital Center, Los Angeles," by D. K. Reynolds, et al. NURS DIG 2:58-65, October, 1974.

"Suicidal patients," by Greer. NM 130:36+, January 16, 1970.

"Suicidal tendencies," SCI N 90:513, December 17, 1966.

"Suicide, a negelected problem," by R. H. Felix. AM J PUBLIC HEALTH 55:16-20, January, 1965.

"Suicide and psychiatric care in the aging," by E. A. Gardner, et al. ARCH GEN PSYCHIAT (CHICAGO) 10:547-553, June, 1964.

"Suicide and psychiatric education," by W. A. Kelly, Jr. AM J PSYCHIAT 130:463-468, April, 1973.

"Suicide and the representation of transparency and cross-sections on the Rorschach," by S. J. Blatt, et al. J CONSULT CLIN PSYCHOL 42:280-287, April, 1974.

"Suicide as catharsis," by J. Slorach. LANCET 2:971, November 4, 1971.

PSYCHIATRY

"Suicide following discharge from psychiatric hospital,"
by I. P. James, et al. ARCH GEN PSYCHIAT (CHICAGO)
10:43-46, January, 1964.

"Suicide for surcease," J MED ASS ALA 34:177-179, December, 1964.

"Suicide in psychiatric patients who have received
hospital treatment," by G. C. Wilson, Jr. AM J PSYCH-
IAT 125:752-757, December, 1968.

"Suicide, lethality, and the psychological autopsy," by
E. S. Shneidman. INT PSYCHIAT CLIN 6:225-250, 1969.

"Suicide, sleep, and death: some possible interrelations
among cessation, interruption, and continuation phenomena," by E. S. Shneidman. J CONSULT PSYCHOL 28:
95-106, April, 1964.

"Survey on suicides and accidental poisoning," by J.
Baker. NT 67:258-261, March 4, 1971.

"The threat of suicide in psychotherapy," by S. Basecu.
AM J PSYCHOTHER 19:99-105, January, 1965.

"Tranquilizers and suicide in the schizophrenic patient,"
by S. Cohen, et al. ARCH GEN PSYCHIAT (CHICAGO) 11:
312-321, September, 1964.

PUBLIC HEALTH
"Emergency services in community mental health," by G.
F. Jacobson. AM J PUBLIC HEALTH 64:24-28, February,
1974.

"Suicide, a public health problem," by L. I. Dublin.
AM J PUBLIC HEALTH 55:12-15, January, 1965.

"Suicide and public health, an attempt at re-conceptual-
ization," by G. M. Crocetti. AM J PUBLIC HEALTH 49:
881-887, July, 1959.

"Suicide as a public health problem," NT 58:889, July
13, 1962.

REHABILITATION: GENERAL

"The chronic wrist-slasher," by Graff. HOSP TOP 45:61+,
November, 1967.

"Durkheim's one cause of suicide," by B. D. Johnson.
AM SOCIOL R 30:875-876, December, 1965.

"Effects of different explanations of disordered behavior on treatment referrals," by C. E. Colson. J CON-
SULT CLIN PSYCHOL 34:432-435, June, 1970.

"Evaluation and treatment of suicide-prone youth," by
M. King.   MENT HYG 55:344-350, July, 1971.

"Keep some hope alive," by Goldfarb. PT CARE 4:119+,
April 15, 1970.

"Learning to live," by R. Dorac.   TIMES ED SUPP 2433:
18, January 5, 1962.

"Movement therapy in the treatment of suicidal patients,"
by M. Chapman.   PERS PSYCHIAT CARE 9:119-122, 1971.

"A program for suicidal patients," by N. Tallent, et
al. AJN 66:2014-2016, September, 1966.

"Recognizing, understanding and treating the suicidal
patient," by Hauser. MED INSIGHT 2:20+, April, 1970.

"Suicide and community care," by D. Walk.   BRIT J
PSYCHIAT 113:1390-1391, December, 1967.

"To live again," by L. David.   GOOD H 175:83+, September, 1972.

"Treating suicide: the illusions of a professional movement (US)," by D. Light, Jr. INTERNAT SOC SCI J 25:
475-488, #4, 1973.

"Up from suicide," CHR TODAY 16:26, June 9, 1972.

"What to do for the suicidal patient," by M. M. Pearson.
MED INSIGHT 5:12-15, March, 1973.

REHABILITATION: MANAGEMENT
  "Classification of suicidal patients," by A. Rosen, et
    al. J CONSULT PSYCHOL 18:359-362, October, 1954.

  "Management of apparent remissions in suicidal patients,"
    by S. Lesse. CURR PSYCHIAT THER 7:73-76, 1967.

  "Management of the presuicidal, suicidal, and post-
    suicidal patient," ANN INTERN MED 75:441-458, Septem-
    ber, 1971.

  "The treatment of the depressed and suicidal geriatric
    patient," by K. Wolff. GERIAT 26:65-69, July, 1971.

RESEARCH
  "Recent research into suicide and attempted suicide,"
    by E. Stengel, et al. J FORENSIC MED 1:252-259,
    July-September, 1954.

  "Rusk analyzes suicide patterns," NEW YORK TIMES 56:4,
    May 19, 1957.

  "Suicide research: a critical review of strategies and
    potentialities in mental hospitals," by M. J. Kahne.
    INT J SOC PSYCHIAT 12:120-129, Spring, 1966.

  "Trends in suicide research," by P. Friedman. MT SINAI
    J MED NY 38:135-147, January-February, 1971.

SOCIOLOGY
  "Attempted suicide in social networks," by N. Kreitman,
    et al. BRIT J PREV SOC MED 23:116-123, May, 1969.

  "Destructive group dynamics: an account of some peculiar
    interrelated incidents of suicide and suicidal attempts
    in a university doemitory," by W. A. Binns, et al.
    J AM COLL HEALTH ASS 14:250-256, April, 1966.

  "Social contexts of suicide," by H. H. Krauss, et al.
    J ABNORM PSYCHOL 78:222-228, October, 1971.

  "Social effects of attempted suicide," by E. Stengel.
    CAN MED ASS J 74:116-120, January 15, 1956.

SOCIOLOGY

"Social factors in suicide," by G. E. Murphy, et al.
JAMA 199:303-308, January 30, 1967.

"The social relations of suicide. The value of a
combined epidemiological and case study approach,"
by P. Sainsbury. SOC SCI MED 6:189-198, April, 1972.

"Sociological aspects of suicide," by D. Szabo. CAN NURS
62:33-38, February, 1966.

"Sociology of suicide prevention: policy implications
of differences between suicidal patients and completed suicides," by R. W. Maris. SOC PROB 17: 132-
149, Summer, 1969.

"Socio-structural analysis of murder, suicide, and
economic crime in Ceylon," by A. L. Wood. AM SOCIOL
R 26:744-753, October, 1961.

STATISTICS

"Alcoholism and suicide rates by status set and occupation," by W. A. Rushing. Q J STUD ALCOHOL 29:399-
412, June, 1968.

"Aspects of the suicide problem (rates and means, 1953-
1955)," MET LIFE STATIS BULL 38:8-10, November, 1957.

"Calculation of some costs of suicide prevention using
certain predictors of suicidal behavior," by J. C.
Diggory. PSYCHOL BULL 71:373-386, May, 1969.

"Completed and attempted suicides: a comparative analysis (based on data for Seattle, Wash., 1948-1952),"
by C. F. Schmid, et al. AM SOCIOL R 20:273-283, June,
1955.

"Cross-validation of the suicidal intent scale," by R.
W. Beck, et al. PSYCHOL REP 34:445-446, April, 1974.

"Deaths by homicide and suicide," SPEC 56-57, November,
1952.

"Demographic factors in suicide in Sweden and in the
United States," by K. E. Rudestam. INT J SOC PSYCH-
IAT 18:79-90, Summer, 1972.

"Differences between national suicide rates," by B. M. Barraclough. BRIT J PSYCHIAT 122:95-96, January, 1973.

"Differences between suicide rates," by P. Sainsbury, et al. NATURE (LONDON) 220:1252, December 21, 1968.

"Firearms and suicide rates," NEW YORK TIMES 6:1, March 30, 1973.

"Increase in suicides in the spring," NEW YORK TIMES 8:1, July 4, 1954.

"International rise in suicide," STATIS BULL METROP LIFE INS CO 48:4-7, March, 1967.

"Measuring the incidence of self-injury: some methodological and design considerations," by P. C. Whitehead, et al. AM J ORTHOPSYCHIAT 43:142-148, January, 1973.

"Mortal statistics," by K. Nott. COMMENTARY 38:64-68, October, 1961. "Reply with rejoinder," by M. L. Farber. 39:6+, April, 1965.

"1952 suicides at all-time low level," SCI N L 64:8, July 4, 1953; SCI DIG 34:33, September, 1953.

"Old and new trends in suicide research," by E. Stengel. BRIT J MED PSYCHOL 33:283-286, 1960.

"Regional variations in mortality from suicide (United States)," METROP STATIS BULL 54:2-4, August, 1973.

"Revised suicide potential scale," by R. W. Miskimins, et al. J CONSULT CLIN PSYCHOL 33:258, April, 1969.

"Rise in frequency of suicide," STATIS BULL METROP LIFE INS CO 45:8-10, July, 1964.

"Seasonal variation in some mental health statistics: suicides, homicides, psychiatric admissions, and institutional placement of the retarded," by G. Cerbus. J CLIN PSYCHOL 26:61-63, January, 1970.

"Some statistics on suicide," by P. H. Martin. J IND
MED ASS   55:85-87, January, 1962.

"Statistical analysis of suicide and other mortality
rates of students," by R. G. Carpenter. BRIT J PREV
SOC MED 13:163-174, October, 1959.

"Statistical aspects," by A. Lewis. CAN MED ASS J 74:
99-104, January 15, 1956.

"Statistics of suicide," SCI DIG 42:28, August, 1957.

"Study of suicide in Philadelphia," by J. Tuckman, et
al. PUBLIC HEALTH REP 73:547-553, June, 1958.

"Suicide among top ten causes of death in U.S.," SCI
DIG 49:24-25, February, 1961.

"Suicide and crime in the social structures of an urban
setting, Fort Worth, Texas 1930-1950," by A. L. Porterfield. AM SOCIOL R 17:341-349, June, 1952.

"Suicide and demography of suicide," by J. Hirsh.
MENT HYG 43:516-525, October, 1959.

"Suicide attempts: validation of the data," by I. Os-
wald, et al. AM J PSYCHIAT 128:900-901, January, 1972.

"Suicide -- international comparisons," METROP LIFE
STATIS BULL 53:2-5, August, 1972.

"Suicide mortality tables(1952-1953) for United States
and Canadian cities," by T. J. V. Cullen. SPEC 107 -
108, May, 1955.

"Suicide rate," by B. M. Barraclough. BRIT MED J 1:293,
February 3, 1973.

"Suicide rate," by B. M. Barraclough. BRIT MED J 3:590,
September 2, 1972.

"Suicide rate," by D. Lester. BRIT MED J 4:612, December 9, 1972.

"Suicide rate at record low," STATIS BULL METROP LIFE
INS CO 34:9-10, May, 1953.

STATISTICS

"Suicide statistics," MEDICOLEG J 37:49-50, 1969.

"Suicide statistics," NEW YORK TIMES 12:2, January 24, 1959.

"Suicide statistics," NEW YORK TIMES 39:3, May 9, 1967.

"Suicide statistics," NEW YORK TIMES 116:6, November 24, 1968.

"Suicide statistics," TIME 61:45, January 5, 1953.

"Suicide tables (1951-1959)," EPIDEMIOL & VITAL STATIS REP 14:144-173, #5, 1961.

"Suicides -- a look at the statistics," by E. T. Dewey. TRANS ASS LIFE INSUR MED DIR AMER 47:54-69, 1964.

"Suicides rising," by D. A. Ehrlich. SCI N 92:229, September 2, 1967.

"World suicide rates," NEW YORK TIMES 6:6, January 12, 1962.

"WORLD SUICIDE RATES," NEW YORK TIMES 2:4, May 5, 1963.

"Young people and suicide rates," NEW YORK TIMES 1:4, April 16, 1973.

STUDENTS: ACHIEVEMENT
"Suicide and educational attainment in a transitional society," by W. L. Li. SOCIOL Q 13:253-258, Spring, 1972.

"Suicide rate greater for more educated," NEW YORK TIMES 19:3, March 18, 1951.

STUDENTS: CHILDREN
SEE: MOTIVATION: CHILDREN

STUDENTS: COLLEGE
"Campus samaritans aid students in distress," by B. Hill. TIMES ED SUPP 2923:12, May 28, 1971.

"Campus suicides," by W. A. Sievert. SAT R ED 1:55, April, 1973.

STUDENTS: COLLEGE

"College suicides," AMERICA 115:502, October 29, 1966.

"Collegians threaten suicide most often," SCI N L 88: 278, October 30, 1965.

"Death on the campus: Oxford and Cambridge," NEWSWEEK 53:69, March 23, 1959.

"Problem of suicide on college campuses," by R. H. Seiden. J SCH HEALTH 41:243-248, May, 1971.

"Signs of suicide: high rate among college students," TIME 91:60, April 12, 1968.

"Student stress, suicide, and the role of the university," by J. M. Whiteley. NAT ASS WOM DEANS & COUNS J 30:120-124, Spring, 1967.

"Suicidal tendencies: college student," TIME 88:114, October 14, 1966.

"What's being done about campus suicide?" by W. Hoffer. ED DIG 38:54-56, October, 1972.

STUDENTS: FORMER COLLEGE
"Chronic disease in former college students precursors of suicide in early and middle life," by R. S. Paffenberger, et al. AM J PUBLIC HEALTH 56: 1026-1036, July, 1966.

STUDENTS: GENERAL
"School age suicide and the educational environment," by F. D. Reese. TIP 7:10-13, February, 1968.

"Student suicide," by S. A. Winickoff, et al. TODAY'S ED 60:30-32+, April, 1971.

"Student suicides," SCI N L 91:45, January 14, 1967.

"Student suicides," by P. Balogh. NEW STATESM 46:591-592, November 14, 1953; "Discussion," 46:637, 673-4, 716+, 761, November 21-December 12, 1953.

"Student suicides," AMERICA 112:344-345, March 13, 1965; "Reply," by D. Brock. 112:470, April 10, 1965.

126

STUDENTS: GENERAL

"Student suicides: end for the uninvolved," CHEM & ENG
N 48:8, April 13, 1970.

"Student suicides mount," SCI DIG 64:65, August, 1968.

"Suicidal students," TIME 80:49, September 7, 1962.

"Suicide and the student," by J. M. Atkinson. UNIV Q
23:213-224, Spring, 1969.

"Suicide and the student," by R. V. Osmon. CONTEMP ED
42:280-283, May, 1971.

"Young people and the suicide rates," NEW YORK TIMES
1:4, April 16, 1973.

SUICIDE: GENERAL
"Adler and the 1910 Vienna Symposium on suicide. A
special review," by H. Ansbacher. J INDIV PSYCHOL 24:
181-192, November, 1968.

"Affective disorder. Diagnostic correlates and incidence of suicide," by F. N. Pitts, Jr., et al. J NERV
MENT DIS 139:176-181, August, 1964.

"Action and reaction in suicidal crisis," by L. J. Mc-
Lean. NURS FORUM 8:28-41, 1969.

"The acute crisis," by C. Coco, et al. PELICAN NEWS 28:
12-15, Winter, 1972.

"Aetiological factors in attempted suicide," by S. Greer,
et al. BRIT MED J 2:1352-1355, December 3, 1966.

"Alive to 45," NT 63:1141-1142, August 25, 1967.

"All that looks like eclampsia . . ." EMERG MED 3:151,
April, 1971.

"An alternative to current analyses of suicidal behavior," by J. K. Mikawa. PSYCHOL REP 32:323-330, February, 1973.

"An analysis of attempted suicide in an urban industrial district," by G. D. Middleton, et al. PRACT
187:776-782, December, 1961.

"An analysis of 500 consecutive patients (other than alcoholics) in an out-patient clinic largely concerned with psychosocial problems," by A. A. Bartholomew, et al. MED J AUST 2:825-827, November 21, 1964.

"An analysis of the sequence of selected events in the lives of a suicidal population: a preliminary report," by J. A. Humphrey, et al. J NERV MENT DIS 154:137-140, February, 1972.

"Anatomy of suicide," by W. B. Dickinson, Jr. ED RES REP 705-722, September 25, 1963.

"The anatomy of suicide," by L. L. Havens. N E J MED 272:401-406, February 25, 1965.

"And certain thoughts through my head," by B. Fallon. AJN 72:1257-1259, July, 1972.

"Anomie and the suicidal individual," by D. Lester. PSYCHOL REP 26:532, April, 1970.

"Anomie my enemy," by D. D. McCall. CHR CENT 85:941-943, July 24, 1968.

"Another look at suicide," by C. M. Wallace. NM 130: 27-28, November 21, 1969.

"Art of suicide," by A. Alvarez. PARTISAN R 37:#3: 339-358, 1970.

"Assessment of suicide," by G. W. Brockopp. PA NURS 25:2-4, December, 1970.

"Attempted suicide in social networks," by N. Kreitman, et al. BRIT J PREV SOC MED 23:116-123, May, 1969.

"Attempted suicide and the experience of violence," by F. A. Whitlock, et al. J BIOSOC SCI 1:353-368, October, 1969.

"Attitudes toward death of NP patients who have attempted suicide," by L. M. Cash, et al. PSYCHOL REP 26: 879-882, June, 1970.

"Autonomic reactivity in relation to the affective meaning of suicide," by D. Spiegel. J CLIN PSYCHOL 25:359-362, October, 1969.

"Barbituates, automatism and suicide," by R. H. Long. POSTGRAD MED 28:A-56-72, October, 1960.

"Basic facts," by O. R. Yost. J S CAROLINA MED ASS 48: 86-93, April, 1952.

"Big bite," by N. Mailer. ESQUIRE 58:168, December, 1962.

"Black suicide: a report of 25 English cases and controls," by C. Bagley, et al. J SOC PSYCHOL 86:175-179, April, 1972.

"Bridge of sighs: Golden Gate," NEWSWEEK 82:61, August 13, 1973.

"Bridge to the mainland," by Bodie. PERS PSYCHIAT CARE 3:8+, #4, 1965.

"The burden of responsibility in suicide and homicide," by P. Solomon. JAMA 199:321-324, January 30, 1967.

"But for the grace of God," NO 13:29+, November, 1965.

"Cartoon appreciation in suicidal and control groups," by P. Keith-Spiegel, et al. J PSYCHIAT RES 8:161-165, June, 1971.

"Case for diagnosis," by P. A. Finck. MILIT MED 135:409-410, May, 1970.

"Case study with particular attention to the 'here-and-now'," by Y. Kunasaka. J EXIST 6:147-160, Winter, 1965-1966.

"Cast off the darkness: condensation," by P. Putnam. LADIES H J 74:68-69+, April, 1957.

"Changing concepts of suicide," JAMA 199:752, March 6, 1967.

SUICIDE: GENERAL

"The crisis treatment of suicide," by N. Tabachnick. NW MED 69:1-8, June, 1970.

"Critical incidents in the context of family therapy," by G. Berenson. INT PSYCHIAT CLIN 7:261-272, 1970.

"Cross-cultural study of the thwarting disorientation theory of suicide," by H. H. Krauss, et al. J ABNORM PSYCHOL 73:353-357, August, 1968.

"Crypto-suicide," by J. Donnelly. MED INSIGHT 5:24-27+, September, 1973.

"Dark side of May," by E. M. Stern. WOM HOME C 78:4+, May, 1951.

"Death by choice," by Kessel. ABBOTTEMPO 3:3+, #2, 1965.

"Death by choice?" by F. J. Moore, et al. J MISS MED ASS 2:593-596, December, 1961.

"Death in the zoo: photograph," TIME 64:14, August 2, 1954.

"Death on the mountain," TIME 71:23, January 13, 1958.

"Depersonalization and self-destruction," by H. Waltzer. AM J PSYCHIAT 125:155-157, September, 1968.

"Deviance, interpersonal relations and suicide," by W. A. Rushing. HUM REL 22:72-75, February, 1969.

"Dichotomous evaluations in suicidal individuals," by C. Neuringer. J CONSULT PSYCHOL 25:445-449, October, 1961.

"The diencephalization of the reactive depression (the suicidal implications of euphemistic names), by J. A. Meerloo. AM J PSYCHIAT 121:376-377, October, 1964.

"The dimensions and dynamics of suicide," by J. Hirsh. ARCH ENVIRON HEALTH (CHICAGO) 2:462-473, April, 1961.

"Disease of self-destruction," by M. Clark. NEWSWEEK 54:61-64, November 2, 1959.

"Clinical and social predictors of repeated attempted suicide; a multivariate analysis," by C. Bagley, et al. BRIT J PSYCHIAT 119:515-521, November, 1971.

"Clinical aspects," by N. Loux. R I MED J 36:248-250, 252, 258, May, 1953.

"Clinical assessment of suicidal risk," by J. Fawcett. POSTGRAD MED 55:85-89, March, 1974.

"Clinical identification of suicidal risk," by G. E. Murphy. ARCH GEN PSYCHIAT 27:356-359, September, 1972.

"Clues to suicide," by J. Strahm. J KANSAS MED SOC 64: 6-8, February, 1963.

"Cognitive complexity of the suicidal individual," by D. Lester. PSYCHOL REP 28:158, February, 1971.

"The cognitive organization of meaning in suicidal individuals," by C. Neuringer. J GENET PSYCHOL 76: 91-100, January, 1967.

"The color-shading response and suicide," by S. Applebaum, et al. J PROJ TECHN 26:155-161, June, 1962.

"Comparative study of suicide," by W. L. Li. INT J COMP SOC 12:281-286, December, 1971.

"Completed suicide and latitude," by D. Lester. PSYCH-OL REP 27:818, December, 1970.

"Completed suicide and longitude," by D. Lester. PSYCH-OL REP 28:662, April, 1971.

"Concerning suicide: anglican committee report," TIME 74:74+, November 2, 1959.

"Contrasting suicide rates in industrial communities," by E. Stengel, et al. J MENT SCI 107:1011-1019, November, 1961.

"Creative suicidal crises," by N. Tabachnick. ARCH GEN PSYCHIAT 29:258-263, August, 1963.

"A follow-up study of 618 suicidal patients," by A. D. Pokorny. AM J PSYCHIAT 122:1109-1116, April, 1966.

"Follow-up study of suicidal patients seen in emergency room consultation," by H. M. Bogard. AM J PSYCHIAT 126:1017-1020, January, 1970.

"From communication to coordination," by Bergman. CAN NURS 63:34+, April, 1967.

"From the cradle to the grave: Denmark," TIME 72:35, November 10, 1958.

"Golden leap," TIME 96:40, August 24, 1970.

"Grim green mountains," TIME 70:28, November 11, 1957.

"A group member's suicide: treating collective trauma," by H. D. Kibel. INT J GROUP PSYCHOTHER 23:42-53, January, 1953.

"Growing problem," by R. A. Kern. CA MED 79:6-10, July, 1953.

"Henry and Short on suicide: a critique," by D. Lester. J PSYCHOL 70:179-186, November, 1968.

"High dive: leaps from Eiffel Tower," NEWSWEEK 61:52, May 20, 1963.

"His canon 'gainst self-slaughter: spies and self-destruction," AMERICA 103:371, June 18, 1960.

"His last card trick," by M. T. Pringle. CORONET 34: 68-69, June, 1953.

"His own executioner," EMERG MED 6:24-30+, January, 1974.

"History in the study of medicine," by G. Rosen. PSYCHOL MED 1:267-285, August, 1971.

"How guilty am I?" NEWSWEEK 47:61, February 20, 1956.

"Human voice means more: means of protest," TIME 86: 118, November 19, 1965.

"Humor and suicide: favorite jokes of suicidal patients," by D. Spiegel, et al. J CONSULT CLIN PSYCHOL 33:504-505, August, 1969.

"I looked down just before I jumped," LIFE 34:28, January 19, 1953.

"I'm going to kill myself," by A. Hamilton. SCI DIG 54: 57-63, September, 1963.

"Immobilization response to suicidal behavior," by R. E. Litman. ARCH GEN PSYCHIAT (CHICAGO) 11:282-285, September, 1964.

"Incidence of suicide," by M. L. Carvey. VA NURS Q 38: 49-53, Summer, 1970.

"An ingenious suicide," MEDICOLEG J 35:73-74, 1967.

"An inquest quashed," by F. A. McLean. LANCET 2:146, July 18, 1970.

"International and cultural conflicts affecting mental health. Violence, suicide and withdrawal," by M. K. Opier. AM J PSYCHOTHER 23:608-620, October, 1969.

"Interpersonal relations in suicidal attempts. Some psychodynamic considerations and implications for treatment," by N. Tabachnick. AMA ARCH GEN PSYCHIAT 4:16-21, January, 1961.

"Interpretations of suicide," by P. Cresswell. BRIT J SOCIOL 23:133-145, June, 1972.

"Invitation to homicide," by L. H. Gold. J FOREN SCI 10:415-421, October, 1965.

"Joke," TIME 62:42, October 19, 1953.

"Joseph in the lion's den," TIME 64:19, July 26, 1954.

"Killers who never go to jail," by M. M. Hunt. SAT EVE POST 226:24-25+, February 6, 1954.

"Lady in the lake: Knoxville, Tenn., " NEWSWEEK 41:56, June 29, 1953.

"Last testament: R. Wishnetsky," NEWSWEEK 67:32, February 28, 1966.

"Learning to live," by R. Dorac. TIMES ED SUPP 2433: 18, January 5, 1962.

"The legacy of suicide. Observations on the pathogenic impact of suicide upon marital partners," by A. C. Cain, et al. PSYCHIAT 29:406-411, November, 1966.

"Letter: L. W. Leslie," TIME 61:31, April 6, 1953.

"Letter from Leete's Island: a case of termination," by J. Fischer. HARPER 246:25-27, February, 1973.

"Letter: obituary date," by K. D. Rose. JAMA 229:521, July 29, 1974.

"Letter: time of death," by J. Fleetwood. BRIT MED J 1:200, February 2, 1974.

"Letter: to be or not to be," by N. F. David. JAMA 226: 468, October 22, 1973.

"Living and dying. Suicide: an invitation to die," by S. M. Jourard. AM J NURS 70:269, February, 1970.

"Love story in Manhattan, TIME 61:21, February 9, 1953.

"A macabre suicide," by H. R. Johnson. MED SCI LAW 7: 210-211, October, 1967.

"A medical approach to suicide prevention," by B. Barraclough. SOC SCI MED 6:661-667, December, 1972.

"Medical contributions to suicide," BRIT MED J 3:610, September 13, 1969.

"Medicolegal and pathologic aspects," by A. E. O'Dea. R I MED J 36:245-247, May, 1953.

"Menoeceus in the Thebaid of Statius," by D. W. Vessey. CLASS PHIL 66:236-243, October, 1971.

"Methodological problems in determining the aetiology of suicide," by G. Simpson. AM SOC R 15:658-663, October, 1950.

"Methodological problems in suicide research," by C. Neuringer. J CONSULT PSYCHOL 26:273-278, June, 1962.

"Methods and fashions of suicide," by J. Hirsh. MENT HYG 44:3-11, January, 1960.

"Mortality from suicide," J FOREN MED 9:1-14, January-March, 1962.

"Mortality from suicide," WHO CHRON 16:15-18, January, 1962.

"Murder or suicide?" by A. Usher. MED SCI LAW 8:260-261, October, 1968.

"Murder or suicide? A case report," by A. Fatteh. J FOREN MED 18:122-123, July-September, 1971.

"My mother's death -- thoughts on being a separate person," by J. Rossner. MS 3:107-108, September, 1974.

"Mythology of suicide," BRIT MED J 1:770, March 28, 1970.

"The need for education on death and suicide," by D. Leviton. J SCH HEALTH 39:270-274, April, 1969.

"Niagara Falls suicides," by D. Lester. JAMA 215:797-798, February 1, 1971.

"Note on status integration and suicide," by R. Hagedorn, et al. SOC PROB 14:79-84, Summer, 1966; "Discussion," 15:510-515, Spring, 1968.

"A note on the possible iatrogenesis of suicide," by J. Andriola. PSYCHIAT 36:213-218, May, 1973.

"No suicide decisions: a procedural rule," by R. Grumet. AM J PSYCHIAT 130:1163, October, 1973.

"Of suicide and folly," CAN MED ASS J 96:1167-1168, April 22, 1967.

"On the communication of suicidal ideas. Some sociological and behavioral considerations," by P. G. Yessler, et al. AMA ARCH GEN PSYCHIAT 3:612-631, December, 1960.

"On the sociology of suicide," by J. M. Atkinson. SOCIOL R 16:83-92, March, 1968.

"On suicide: Time essay," TIME 88:48-49, November 25, 1966.

"On suicide: reflections upon Camus' view of the problem," by J. J. Kockelmans. PSYCHOANAL R 54:31-48, Fall, 1967.

"Our role in the generation, modification, and termination of life," by R. H. Williams. TRANS ASS AM PHYS 82:1-22, 1969.

"Pacific dialectic," by P. Burnham. COMMONWEAL 70:274, June 12, 1959.

"Peace suicides: Joan Fox and Craig Badiali of Blackwood, N.J.," by E. Asinof. SEVENTEEN 29:174+, March, 1970.

"The personal future and suicidal ideation," by F. T. Melges, et al. J NERV MENT DIS 153:244-250, October, 1971.

"Post mortem," by Strix. SPEC 196:47, January 13, 1956.

"The problem of suicide in general practice," by C. A. Watts. PROC ROY SOC MED 54:264-266, April, 1961.

"Producing suicides," by J. L. Wilkins. AM BEHAV SCI 14:185-201, November, 1970.

"A prospective study of the Rorshachs of suicides:
the predictive potential of pathological content,"
by C. B. Thomas, et al. JOHNS HOPKINS MED J 132:
334-360, June, 1973.

"Provocation of suicide attempts," by C. H. Fellner.
J NERV MENT DIS 132: 334-360, June, 1973.

"A psychiatric approach to the diagnosis of suicide
and its effect upon the Edinburgh statistics," by
I. M. Ovenstone. BRIT J PSYCHIAT 123:21, July, 1973.

"The psychodynamics of suicide," by S. S. Furst, et al.
BULL N Y ACAD MED 41:190-204, February, 1965.

"Psychological-psychiatric aspects in certifying modes
of death,' by R. E. Litman. J FORNSIC SCI 13:46-54,
January, 1969.

"Public conceptions and attitudes about suicide," by G.
P. Ginsburg. J HEALTH SOC BEHAV 12:200-207, September,
1971.

"Public health and the law. Suicide: civil right or
punishable crime?" by W. J. Curran. AM J PUBLIC HEALTH
60:163-164, January, 1970.

"Quadruple suicide," NEW YORK TIMES 33:2, December 1,
1958.

"Quiet cries. Can I help? Will you listen?" by M. Heath.
NURS CARE 6:26-29+, April, 1973.

"Recent trends in suicide," STATIS BULL METROP LIF INS
CO 51:10-11, May, 1970.

"Remedying a misidentification," by G. Thurston. MED LEG
J 39:31, 1971.

"Relation of suicide rates to social conditions (by age,
sex, race)," by B. MacMahon, et al. PUBLIC HEALTH REP
78:285-293, April, 1963.

"A repertory grid study of the meaning and consequences
of a suicidal act," by A. Ryle. BRIT J PSYCHIAT 113:
1393-1403, December, 1967.

"A review of 139 suicidal gestures: discussion of some
psychological implications and treatment techniques,"
by J. H. Newby, Jr., et al. MILIT MED 133:629-637,
August, 1968.

"Risk-rescue ratingin suicide assessment," by A. D.
Weisman, et al. ARCH GEN PSYCHIAT 26:553-560, June,
1972.

"Self-destructiveness and self-preservation," by E.
Stengel. CLIN MED 69:2275-2279, October, 1962.

"Self-destructiveness and self-preservation," by E.
Stengel. BULL MENINGER CLIN 26:7-17, January, 1962.

"Self-injury. Identification and intervention," by F. G.
Johnson, et al. CAN PSYCHIAT ASS J 18:101-105, April,
1973.

"Self-poisoning," by N. Kessel. BRIT MED J 5473:1265-
1270, November, 1965.

"The semantic differential as an indicator of suicidal
behavior and tendencies," by K. P. Blau, et al.
PSYCHOL REP 21:609-612, October, 1967.

"Shadow of a leap," LIFE 36:28, February 1, 1954.

"Social contexts of suicide," by H. H. Krauss, et al.
J ABNORM PSYCHOL 78:222-228, October, 1971.

"Social effects of attempted suicide," by E. Stengel.
CAN MED ASS J 74:116-120, January 15, 1956.

"Social factors in suicide," by G. E. Murphy, et al.
JAMA 199:303-308, January 30, 1967.

"Somatic suicide, total and partial," by K. Menninger.
BULL MENNINGER CLIN 37:341-354, July, 1973.

"Some explanations for 'unexplained mental phenomena regarding suicide'," by K. R. Wurtz. J NERV MENT DIS 129:578-580, December, 1959.

"A report on psychiatric emergencies," by A. Miller. CAN HOSP 36:36-37, December, 1959.

"Structural analysis of suicidal behavior," by G. Lanteri-Laura, et al. SOC RES 37:324-347, Autumn, 1970.

"Structural change and the Durkheimian legacy: a macro-social analysis of suicide rates," by J. D. Miley, et al. AM J SOC 78:657-673, November, 1972.

"Study of social and psychological characteristics of adolescent suicide attempters in an urban disadvantaged area," by B. F. Corder, et al. ADOLESCENCE 9: 1-6, Spring, 1974.

"A study of suicide pacts," by J. Cohen. MEDICOLEG J 29:144-151, 1961.

"A study of the suicide problem in the emergency suite of university hospital," by L. W. Blunt, et al. UNIV MI MED BULL 29:155-164, May-June, 1963.

"Successful suicide in a patient with conversion reaction," by J. H. Satterfield. AM J PSYCHIAT 118: 1047-1048, May, 1962.

"Suicidal attempts in psychomotor epilepsy," by. G. Anastassopoulos, et al. BEHAV NEUROPSYCHIAT 1:11-16, December, 1969.

"Suicidal behavior," by J. Wilkins. AM SOC R 32:286-298, April, 1967.

"Suicidal behavior: assaultiveness , and socialization principles," by J. E. Teele. SOC FORCES 43:510-518, May, 1965.

"Suicidal behavior. Distinction in patients with sedative poisoning seen in a general hospital," by P. R. McHugh, et al. ARCH GEN PSYCHIAT 25:456-464, November, 1971.

"Suicidal ideation and behavior in a general population,"
by J. J. Schwab, et al. DIS NERV SYST 33:745-748,
November, 1972.

"Suicidal ignorance re: suicide," SCI DIG 72:55, August,
1972.

"The suicidal patient in the general hospital," by E.
Stengel. NT 59:1083-1084, August, 1963.

"Suicidal responses on Rorshach test: validation report;
protocols of suicidal mental hospital patients com-
pared with those of nonsuicidal patients," by G. A.
Sakheim. J NERV & MENT DIS 122:332-344, October, 1955.

"Suicide,' by J. Choron. HARPER 244:102-105, June, 1972.

"Suicide," ECONOMIST 182:803, March 9, 1957.

"Suicide," by A. Giddens. BRIT J SOC 16:164-165, June,
1965.

"Suicide," by P. C. Hoaken. CAN MED ASS J 106:854, April
22, 1972.

"Suicide," by D. D. Jackson. SCI AM 191:88-92+, November, 1954.

"Suicide," LANCET 1:508, March 8, 1969.

"Suicide," by D. Lester. J MED SOC NJ 64:665-667, August, 1972.

"Suicide," by P. M. Margolis. UNIV MI MED CENT J 35:10-
12, January-March, 1969.

"Suicide," MD MED 13:85, November, 1964.

"Suicide," by Poulos. BED NURS 3:26+, January, 1970.

"Suicide," by R. M. Steinhilber. MINN MED 51:1205,
September, 1968.

"Suicide," TIME 68:355, August 13, 1956.

"Suicide," by Wallace. NM 127:16, August 30, 1968.

"Suicide," by J. M. Weiss. PSYCHIAT Q 28:250-252, April, 1954.

"Suicide," by P. Wyden. SAT EVE POST 234:18-19+, August 19, 1961.

"Suicide: a continuing problem," by M. J. Martin. J IOWA MED SOC 55:533-536, September, 1965.

"Suicide: a critical review of the literature," by K. S. Adam. CAN PSYCHIAT ASS J 12:413-420, August, 1967.

"Suicide and crime in folk and in secular society," by A. L. Porterfield. AM J SOCIOL 57:331-338, January, 1952.

"Suicide and social isolation," by E. Stengel. 20TH CENT 173:24-36+, Summer, 1964.

"Suicide as a dying art," by D. Norwood. N AM R 2:21-22, November, 1965.

"Suicide: a cultural and semantic view," by W. H. Urban. MENT HYG 46:377-381, July, 1962.

"Suicide: a neglected problem," by C. H. Fellner. AM PRACT 12:283-285, April, 1961.

"Suicide: a new attack against an old killer," by J. Star. LOOK 30:62+, August 23, 1966.

"Suicide: a public health problem," by L. I. Dublin. AM J PUBLIC HEALTH 55:12-15, January, 1965.

"Suicide among the sick in classical antiquity," by. D. Gourevitch. BULL HIST MED 43:501-518, November-December, 1969.

"Suicide: an epidemiological study," by L. Spalt, et al. DIS NERV SYST 33:23-29, January, 1972.

"Suicide and assessing its risk," by R. B. Garnand.
ROCKY MOUNTAIN MED J 63:55-57, November, 1966.

"Suicide and community care," by D. Walk. BRIT J PSYCH-
IAT 113:1381-1391, December, 1967.

"Suicide and euthanasia," by D. A. Roche. BRIT MED J
3:50, July 3, 1971.

"Suicide and euthanasia," by H. Trowell. BRIT MED J
2:275, May 1, 1971.

"Suicide and marital status: a changing relationship?"
by J. Rico-Velasco, et al. J MARRIAGE & FAM 35:239-
244, May, 1973.

"Suicide and nonymity," by J. Wilkins. PSYCHIAT 32:303-
312, August, 1969.

"Suicide and related clinical problems," by C. P. Malm-
quist. MINN MED 52:1597-1602, October, 1969.

"Suicide and self-assult: an introductory course for
medical students," by E. Cohen. J MED ED 49:383-385,
April, 1974.

"Suicide and systematic desensitization: a case study,"
by T. N. Elliott, et al. J CLIN PSYCHOL 28:420-423,
July, 1972.

"Suicide and the Ajax of Sophocles," by M. D. Faber.
PSYCHOANAL R 54:49-60, Fall, 1967.

"Suicide and the fatal accidents act," BRIT MED J 5198:
610, August 20, 1960.

"Suicide and the welfare state," by M. L. Farber. MENT
HYG 49:371-373, July, 1965.

"Suicide as a complication to group psychotherapy," by
J. L. McCartney. MILIT MED 126:895-989, December, 1961.

"Suicide as a dying art," by D. Norwood. N AM R 2:21-22, November, 1965.

"Suicide as communication: Adler's concept and current applications," by H. L. Ansbacher. J INDIV PSYCHOL 25:174-180, November, 1969.

"Suicide as seen in poison control centers," by M. S. McIntire, et al. PEDIAT 48:914-922, December, 1971.

"Suicide. Clues from interpersonal communication," by J. Fawcett, et al. ARCH GEN PSYCHIAT (CHICAGO) 21: 129-137, August, 1969.

"Suicide -- dangerous six weeks," PHYS WORLD 2:19, April, 1967.

"Suicide, homicide and the effects of socialization," by D. Lester. J PERSON SOC PSYCHOL 5:466-468, April, 1967.

"Suicide, homicide, and the socialization of aggression," by M. Gold. AM J SOC 63:651-661, May, 1958.

"Suicide, hysteria, and conversion symptoms," by S. B. Guze. JAMA 225:65, July 2, 1973.

"Suicide in a heterogeneous society," by B. Modan, et al. BRIT J PSYCHIAT 116:65-68, January, 1970.

"Suicide in identical twins," by D. W. Swanson. AM J PSYCHIAT 116:934-935, April, 1960.

"Suicide in professional groups," by P. H. Blachly, et al. N E J MED 268:1278-1282, June 6, 1963.

"Suicide in the subway. Publicly witnessed attempts of 50 cases," by F. G. Guggenheim, et al. J NERV MENT DIS 155:404-409, December, 1972.

"Suicide in today's society," by E. Cunningham. MED J AUST 2:1197-1200, December 28, 1968.

"Suicide in today's society," by E. C. Dax. MED J AUST 1:425, February 22, 1969.

"Suicide in today's society," by F. A. Whitlock. MED J AUST 1:361-362, February 15, 1969.

"Suicide is dangerous,' by L. David. CORONET 37:157-160, February, 1955.

"Suicide: need for a significant other," by E. T. Culver. CHR CENT 86:100-102, January 15, 1969.

"Suicide; Part 3, dynamics of suicide," by J. Hirsh. MENT HYG 44:274-280, April, 1960.

"Suicide: the opaque act," by P. F. Eggertsen. MILIT MED 132:9-17, January, 1967.

"Suicide problem in French sociology," by A. Giddens. BRIT J SOC 16:318, March, 1965.

"The suicide problem up to date," by E. Stengel. CURR MED DRUGS 6:3-17, February, 1966.

"Suicide rate. A problem of validity and comparability," by W. B. Donovan, et al. MARQUETTE MED REV 27:150-158, March, 1962.

"Suicide scare," by D. Gould. NEW STATESM 82:430-431, October 1, 1971.

"Suicide takes a holiday," AMERICA 104:411, December 24, 1960.

"Suicide that lives in all of us: report of a symposium held in Washington," by L. Wainwright. LIFE 59:26, October 29, 1965.

"Suicide: the clinical problem," by D. Maddison, et al. BRIT J PSYCHIAT 112:693-702, July, 1966.

"Suicide -- the deserted field," by J. H. Brown. CAN PSYCHIATR ASS J 18:93-94, April, 1973.

"Suicide.   The nondiminishing rate," by R. Harris. MINN
MED   51:723-726, May, 1968.

"Suicide -- to be or not to be," by A. C. Neiswander. J
AM INST HOMEOP 58:42-45, January-February, 1965.

"Suicides -- does our society care?" by J. Halick. MI
MED 71:325-326, April, 1972.

"Suicides in medical and surgical wards of general
hospitals," by R. J. Stoller, et al. J CHRON DIS 12:
592-599, December, 1960.

"Suicidology," by M. Fishbein.   POSTGRAD MED 45:229,
February, 1969.

"Survey on suicides and accidental poisoning," by J.
Baker.   NT 67:258-261, March 4, 1971.

"Taste of hemlock," TIME 99:85+, June 12, 1972.

"The taxonomy of suicide as seen in poison control centers," by M. S. McIntire, et al. PEDIAT CLIN N AM 17:
697-706, August, 1970.

"Temporal orientation in suicidal patterns," by G.
Greaves.   PERCEPT MOT SKILLS   33:1020, December, 1971.

"Temporal perspective and completed suicide," by D.
Lester.   PERCEPT MOT SKILLS 36:760, June, 1973.

"Texas plane crash: nonviolent man's final act brings
destruction and death," by P. R. Winklemann.   CHR
CENT 88:26+, January 6, 1971.

"A textbook of medicine in general practice.   The suicide problem in general practice," by E. Stengel.
MED WORLD (LONDON) 99:21-24, May, 1963.

"Theory of status integration and its relationship to
suicide," by J. P. Gibbs, et al. AM SOC R 23:140-
147, April, 1958.

"Threat," by R. W. Garnett, Jr. VA MED MONTH 80:455-
458, August, 1953.

"Threat," by L. J. Siegal, et al. DIS NERV SYST 16:37-46, February, 1955.

"Three days to resolve a crisis," EMERG MED 2:58+, August, 1970.

"A time to die," by W. R. Lewis. NURS FORUM 4:7-26, 1965.

"To live again," by L. David. GOOD H 175:83+, September, 1972.

"Toward understanding suicide,' by R. Noyes, Jr. J IOWA MED SOC 58:1147-1152, November, 1968.

"Traitor within," by E. R. Ellis, et al. CATH WORLD 195:377-378, September, 1972.

"Treatment of the hospitalized patient," by A. A. Stone. CURR PSYCHIAT THER 9:209-217, 1969.

"Under the cover of his charm," by P. O. Radulovic. AJN 73:1731-1737, October, 1973.

"Until death ensues," by B. A. Davis. NURS CLIN N AM 7:303-309, June, 1972.

"Ultimately sorrowful," CHR CENT 84:1415, November 1, 1967.

"Up from suicide," CHR TODAY 16:26, June 9, 1972.

"VNA conference on suicide, April 15-16, 1970; summary and closing remarks," by M. Lohr. VA NURS Q 38:55-57, Summer, 1970.

"Violence towards self. A study in suicide," by W. E. Sorrel. DIS NERV SYST 33:501-508, August, 1972.

"Way of suicide," NEWSWEEK 71:97, April 1, 1968.

"We all make mistakes," NM 135:8, December 22, 1972.

"Welfare, suicide linked?" SCI N L 88:111, August 14, 1965.

SUICIDE: GENERAL

"What about suicide?"   AMERICA 103:591, September 3,
1960.

"When patients commit suicide," by R. E. Litman.   AM
J PSYCHOTHER 19:570-576, October, 1965.

"While of unsound sales," by V. Brome.   NEW STATESM 87:
656, May 10, 1974.

"Who commits suicide?"   POSTGRAD MED 43:198, June, 1968.

"Wishes for life and death of some patients who attempted
suicide," by P. E. Sisneos, et al. MENT HYG 46:543-552,
October, 1962.

"Women suicides increase due to social pressures," SCI
N L   85:271, April 25, 1964.

TABOO
"The present suicide taboo in the United States,"   by C.
J. Frederick.   MENT HYG 55:178-183, April, 1971.

"The taboo of suicide," by R. Noyes, Jr. PSYCHIAT 31:173-
183, May, 1968.

TELEPHONE
"An analysis of suicide calls received by a personal
emergency advisory (telephone) service," by A. A.
Bartholomew, et al. MED J AUST 2:488-492, September
21, 1963.

"Anonymous suicidal telephone calls: a research critique,"
by N. Tabachnick, et al. PSYCHIAT 33:526-532, November, 1970.

"Chronic callers to a suicide prevention center," by
D. Lester, et al.   COMM MENT HEALTH J 6:246-250, June,
1970.

"The clients of the telephone samaritan service in Western Australia," by R. A. Finlay-Jones, et al. MED J
AUST 1:690-694, April 1, 1972.

"Dial Mansion House 9000.   The samaritans," by E. Anstice. NT 63:123-124, January 27, 1967.

"ED telephone: a lifeline for potential suicides."
by H. L. Resnik, et al. RN 37:OR/ED 1-2+, October,
1974.

"Fake suicide calls," SCI N L 89:278, April 16, 1966.

"A follow-up study of those who called a suicide prevention center," by J. Wilkins. AM J PSYCHIAT 127:
155-161, August, 1970.

"Geographical location of callers to a suicide prevention
center: note on the evaluation of suicide prevention
programs," by D. Lester. PSYCHOL REP 28:421-422,
April, 1971.

"I don't know why I'm calling, nobody can help me," by
B. Asbell. REDBOOK 135:53+, June, 1970.

"No name -- a study of anonymous suicidal telephone
calls," by N. Tabachnick, et al. PSYCHIAT 28:79-
87, February, 1965.

"A phone call away," by P. Clemmons. Q REV DC NURS ASS
39:3-6, Summer, 1971.

"Phone suicide warnings are calls for help," SCI N L
79:361, June 10, 1961.

"Special 24-hour phone service to curb suicides," NEW
YORK TIMES 8:4, August 28, 1963.

"Suicide calls and identification of suicidal callers,"
by J. Wilkins. MED J AUST 2:923-929, October 21,
1972.

"Suicide prevention telephone service," by Litman.
JAMA 192:107+, April 5, 1965.

"Telephone appraisal of 100 suicidal emergencies," by
M. N. Kaplan, et al. AM J PSYCHOTHER 16:591-599,
October, 1962.

"Who calls the suicide prevention center: a study of
55 persons calling on their own behalf," by G. E.
Murphy, et al. AM J PSYCHIAT 126:314-324, September,
1969.

U.S.A.: ALABAMA

U.S.A.: ALABAMA
  "Suicide in Birmingham," by C. Hassall, et al.
    BR MED J 1:717-8, March 18, 1972.

U.S.A.: ALASKA
  "Suicide and culture in Fairbanks: a comparison
    of three cultural groups in a small city of in-
    terior Alaska," by M. Parkin. PSYCHIATRY 37:60-
    7, February, 1974.

U.S.A.: CALIFORNIA
  "Eerie encounter in wonderful San Francisco," by
    H. Borovik. ATLAS 15:37-9, March, 1968.

  "Study of suicides in Los Angeles and Vienna," by
    N. L. Farberow, et al. PUB HEALTH REPTS 84:389-
    403, May, 1969.

  "Suicide among Chinese in San Francisco," by P. G.
    Bourne. AM J PUBLIC HEALTH 63:744-50, August,
    1973.

  "Suicide in San Francisco: reported and unreported,"
    by E. Cohen. CALIF MED 102:426-30, June, 1965.

  "Suicide in San Francisco's skid row," by C. C.
    Attkisson. ARCH GEN PSYCHIAT (Chicago) 23:149-
    57, August, 1970.

  "Suicides in San Mateo County," by G. Krieger.
    CALIF MED 107:153-5, August, 1967.

U.S.A.: COLORADO
  "Suicide rates in Boulder County, Colorado. Impli-
    cations for physicians," by E. Lang, et al. ROCKY
    MT MED J 69:33-8, December, 1972.

U.S.A.: FLORIDA
  "Suicide in Dade County, Florida," by A. F. Schiff.
    MED TIMES 92:977-9, October, 1964.

U.S.A.: GENERAL
  "Over 19,000 suicides in the United States," by
    Van Itallie. PULSE 17:3+, #3, 1963.

U.S.A.: GENERAL

"Present suicide taboo in the United States," by
    C. J. Frederick. MENT HY 55:178-83, April, 1971.

"Southern suicide statistics," by A. L. Porterfield.
    AM SOCIOL R 14:481-90, August, 1949.

"Southern violence," by S. Hackney. AM HIST R
    74:906-25, February, 1969.

"Suicide in the United States," by J. T. Massey.
    VITAL HEALTH STATIST 20:1-34, August, 1967.

"Suicide takes an American life every 26 minutes,"
    by Golin. PN 13:30+, September, 1963.

U.S.A.: HAWAII
    "Japanese suicides in Hawaii 1958-1969," by D.
    Lum. HAWAII MED J 31:19-23, January-February,
    1972.

U.S.A.: ILLINOIS
    "Suicide in Chicago: a call for action," by T.
    Kostrubala. ILLINOIS MED J 130:54-5, July, 1966.

    "Suicide in Illinois," by J. Baar. CHICAGO MED
    63:13-4, June, 1961.

    "Suicide, status, and mobility in Chicago," by
    R. Maris. SOC FORCES 46:246-56, December, 1967.

U.S.A.: KANSAS
    "Suicide--in the Kansas City area: a pilot study,"
    by R. E. Bidwell, et al. J KANSAS MED SOC 69:
    106-13, March, 1968.

U.S.A.: LOUISIANA
    "Suicide, migration, and race: a study of cases in
    New Orleans," by W. Breed. J SOC ISSUES 22:30-43,
    January, 1966.

U.S.A.: MICHIGAN
    "Suicide: an instance of high rural rates (data
    from a study of male suicides in Michigan, 1945-
    1949)," by W. W. Schroeder, et al. RURAL SOCIOL
    18:45-52, March, 1953.

U.S.A.: NEBRASKA

U.S.A.: NEBRASKA
"Death by their own hands--a statistical study of
suicides in Nebraska during 1968," by A. M.
Reeve. NEBR STATE MED J 55:680-3, November, 1970.

"A ten-year survey of suicide in Omaha-Douglas
County, Nebraska," by B. Tunakan, et al. NEBR
MED J 57:265-9, July, 1972.

U.S.A.: NEW HAMPSHIRE
"A comparison of suicide victims and suicide at-
tempters in New Hampshire," by B. E. Segal, et al.
DIS NERV SYST 31:830-8, December, 1970.

U.S.A.: NEVADA
"Suicide in Nevada. A comparative analysis," by
J. Mikawa, et al. ROCKY MT MED J 70:43-9,
March, 1973.

U.S.A. OKLAHOMA
"On suicide rate differentials in Tulsa," by B.
Brenner. AM SOCIOL R 25:265-6, April, 1960.

U.S.A.: SOUTH CAROLINA
"Suicide in South Carolina, 1955-1966," by R. L.
McCurdy, et al. J S CAROLINA MED ASS 65:76-80,
March, 1969.

U.S.A.: TEXAS
"Suicide and crime in the social structure of an
urban setting: Fort Worth, 1930-1950," by A. L.
Porterfield. AM SOCIOL R 17:341-9, June, 1952.

U.S.A.: VIRGINIA
"Suicide in Virginia and the nation," by M. Shan-
holtz. VIRGINIA MED MONTHLY 95:583-4, September,
1968.

"Suicides in Virginia," by I. H. Sie. VIRGINIA MED
MONTHLY 92:370-6, August, 1965.

U.S.A.: WASHINGTON
"A study of suicide in King County, Washington,"
by T. L. Dorpat, et al. NORTHWEST MED 61:655-
61, August, 1962.

U.S.A.: WASHINGTON

  "A study of suicide in the Seattle area," by T. L.
   Dorpat, et al. COMPR PSYCHIAT 1:349-59, December,
   1960.

U.S.A.: WEST VIRGINIA
  "Deaths by suicide in West Virginia (1960)," by
   N. H. Dyer, et al. W VIRGINIA MED J 58:114-5, May,
   1962.

AUTHOR INDEX